HOW TO BECOME A WORLD-CLASS INVESTIGATOR

HOW TO BECOME A WORLD-CLASS INVESTIGATOR

AN INSIDER'S GUIDE TO A SECRETIVE INDUSTRY

JULIE CLEGG

LIONCREST
PUBLISHING

HOW TO BECOME A WORLD-CLASS INVESTIGATOR
An Insider's Guide to a Secretive Industry

ISBN   978-1-5445-1209-9 *Paperback*
       978-1-5445-1210-5 *Ebook*

For Stephanie, my inspiration and my purpose.

CONTENTS

INTRODUCTION

Change in the world always begins with an individual who shares what he or she has learned and passes it on to others.

—DALAI LAMA

Are you naturally drawn to the thrill of investigations, but you have no idea how to break into the industry? You're not alone. I've spent more than two decades in this field as a detective on a police force, an educator, a profiler, a technologist, and a professional investigator, and I can tell you that everyone's story of what leads them into this industry is different. Why? Because there's no template for entering the investigation field.

Let me tell how I got into investigations. As you read through my story, I want you to ask yourself a question: "Could this be me?"

A PATTERN FROM CHAOS

As a teenager growing up in the West Yorkshire town of Bradford, England, I read books voraciously. I fell in love with the English language and writing. I carried books with me wherever I went, pursuing words with a passion. My mom would say to me, "You know, Julie, you've always got your nose in a book." And she was right. Books were my escape.

Every Saturday morning, for years, I descended into the dingy underground market in Shipley, where there was an amazing bookstore. The storekeeper would set aside books that he knew I'd like—sometimes Stephen King, other times Sherlock Holmes or Nancy Drew—and I'd trade in my previous week's books for others.

This love of reading led me to a fascination with journalism. As a youth, I read because I wanted to learn how to write well, but as I grew into young adulthood, I found myself getting lost in the mysteries and in the investigation work of the characters.

For two years as a young teenager, in order to indulge my passion for reading, as well as meet my school and studying obligations, I set up a timetable on my bedroom wall for reading and homework. I sat in my bedroom watching my friends hanging out in the streets while I studied. That's just who I was—diligent, tenacious, and organized.

Even then, I was able to put aside my social needs to focus on what needed to be done—to a fault. Later, I would receive a comment in my police training binder that said, "Julie needs to learn to let things go."

This feedback was meant to indicate an area of potential improvement for me. However, my tenacity and perfectionism were two of the earliest signs that I was destined to be a world-class investigator, along with my love of problem-solving. As a young child, I would sit on our Tarmac driveway and pull out the little decorative white stones for hours on end, then try to find the patterns in the shapes to fit them back into their original holes.

I didn't realize it at the time, but everything I did—even pulling stones from the driveway—was a form of analytics. To me, problem-solving has always been a game, an unconscious way of finding answers to the question, "How do I decipher a pattern from chaos?"

BOXING DAY

On Boxing Day, when I was seventeen, I was the victim of a violent sexual assault—to the point that I was almost killed. The detective assigned to my case was a woman named Diane Watts. As a teenaged victim of a vicious assault, Diane was like an angel to me. The first thing she said when I went down to the police station was,

"I've been told what happened. I want you to know that I believe you."

I still get emotional thinking about her words to me that horrific day. It had never crossed my mind that someone wouldn't believe me, but hearing her say those words sent a wave of relief through my body. She asked me what I needed. I was in such shock that I didn't know how to answer.

"When was the last time you ate?" she asked.

I didn't even know what day it was. "I have no idea," I said.

Diane ordered me a pizza. She held my hand during my medical examination. She took down my thirty-seven-page statement without a hint of hurry or frustration. They were such small, simple gestures, yet everything down to the way she asked questions told me that she cared. She never made me feel questioned; she was just trying to pull out the information necessary to help her solve the case.

Even after the incident, Diane kept in touch with me, calling me up to make sure I was doing all right. "Anytime you need to talk," she said, "here's my personal number. I'm here for you."

Her professionalism and kindness shattered all of the impressions I had of detectives up to that point, which I only knew from detective novels, where everyone was hard-nosed and typically male. She was the most inspiring person I'd ever met. I know I would have recovered either way, but if somebody else had been assigned to my case, my emotional recovery would have taken much longer. She made the whole process bearable. Because of the positive way she handled my case and her incredible support afterward, I realized I wanted to spend my life helping people the way Diane had helped me.

YOU'RE SAFE HERE

Initially, the police force rejected me. After meeting Diane, I felt like I'd finally found my calling in life. Coming out on the other side of that assault, I realized what I was capable of—what I was able to survive. I knew I wanted to be a police officer, but at eighteen years old, just a year after that almost-fatal assault, they told me I needed more confidence and experience. I was devastated.

But I always bounce back. I set out to gain more life experience by getting out of my comfort zone as an introvert and working in the bar and nightclub industry. My confidence soared. I worked long hours. I had to break up fights. I gained experience dealing with the police, who'd come to the bars and clubs on the lookout for gangs and drug dealers.

After three years of mastering the seedy, crime-ridden world of nightclubs in the old mill town of Bradford, England, I went back to reapply for the police, now different and more experienced. This time they hired me.

On my first day at the police station that I had been assigned to, they showed all of us—the brand-new uniformed bobbies on the beat—around the station. Upstairs, where the detectives worked, the walls were plastered with maps and pictures of crime scenes connected by strings. To a rookie like me, I felt as though I'd stepped into a scene from a movie. After all I had been through, I couldn't believe I was finally a part of this.

Then I turned around and saw Diane standing there. I froze in place. In an instant, my memory flashed back to that Boxing Day almost five years earlier when she'd supported me through the darkest days of my life. A mix of fear and comfort coursed through me; part of me wanted to run away, and the rest wanted to run toward her at the same time. Diane personified the memory of my assault—something I'd kept secret for so long—but she also exuded warmth and nurturance. My past stared back at me in the form of Diane.

After my momentary shock wore off, I realized something both disappointing and relieving—she didn't recognize me. Here in front of me was the person who embodied everything I'd tried to become since that Boxing Day. I wanted her to see me as a peer, not a victim. So I said nothing, hoping she'd forgotten who I was.

Eventually, I was partnered with Diane and sent on patrol to shadow her and learn the ropes. I introduced myself at the start of the morning, but there was no sign of recognition on her face.

Later that morning, out of the blue, as we drove along, she said, "By the way, I anonymized your file."

"What do you mean?" I asked.

"I didn't want anybody to know who you are and have that affect your career, so I removed your identity from your file and all of the evidence that was with it."

I thought of all the forensic evidence I knew had been in there—and the photographs.

"You don't need to worry about anybody knowing what happened," she continued. "You're safe here."

I was shocked that she'd not only recognized me but that

she'd taken the steps to protect me without being asked to. I'd never met anyone in my life before who was so deeply human, with caring, empathy, and integrity guiding her every move.

A KICK IN MY BELLY

One of my last cases as a detective, after many years of working my way through various specialized departments in the police, was a missing-person case. I happened to be pregnant at the time. My superiors had told me to go on light duties, but I said, "I'm pregnant, not sick. I am continuing to do my job."

Diane and I were paired together for this case. We made a great team. I followed her lead, and she mentored me along the way. It was a perfect dynamic for that time in my career. As part of our investigation, we visited the house of the sister of the man who'd gone missing. At the time, I was only about five months pregnant, so my bump wasn't really showing.

We told the woman that her brother Michael might have gone missing under suspicious circumstances, which is why she had two detectives in her house rather than uniformed police officers. Here we were, having this very serious, somber conversation, when all of a sudden, my baby kicked for the first time. Diane noticed the change in my face. Being the professional she was, she didn't say anything, but when we got out to the car, she asked me what had happened.

"I think my baby's kicking," I said.

"That's amazing!" Diane said. "We have to tell her."

I pleaded with Diane not to go back and tell this woman whose brother just went missing that my baby had kicked for the first time. Diane could not be persuaded. She jumped out of the car, knocked on the door, and said, "I just want to tell you that in the midst of all of this sadness and terrible situation that's happening to you, Julie's baby just kicked for the first time while we were in your house. I just wanted to share that with you because it's so joyful."

And you know what? The woman was thrilled. She was so excited that she came running out to the car to congratulate me. That was just Diane. She was intuitively human and compassionate. She never lost sight of the fact that investigative work will always be deeply human. I knew then that I was on the right path. I'd taken the step to become a police officer, I'd had this incredible gift of working with Diane, and I could see in her the future version of myself. At the time, however, I had no idea just how far her mentorship would help propel me in my career. First, she was my role model, then she was my mentor, then she was my peer, and there, in that moment when she ran up to tell that missing man's sister that my baby kicked, she was an incredible human being—as simple and profound as that was.

We threw everything into that case. We hiked down ravines, clambered up hillsides, and climbed fences looking for Michael. When we finally found his body, he was floating in a canal. I can still see him in my memory, all the way down to the jacket he was wearing. His sister invited Diane and me to his funeral and thanked us in front of everybody for our work on the case.

By then, I was heavily pregnant with a big belly. Michael's sister felt such a connection with Diane and me that she gave us both gold bracelets and gave me a teddy bear. "This is for your baby," she said. That teddy bear, which I named Michael, still sits on my bed as a reminder, every single day, that the work I do is intrinsically human.

HUNTED

After working in the police service in Bradford for many years, I took a leave of absence and left England to build on my experience in the internet intelligence field in Canada. I joined a company that trained law enforcement officers, government officials, and military personnel around the world on how to use the internet as a means of investigation (this was in 2004, when all of this was still new to most people). Eventually, I decided to stay in Canada and resigned from the police force, which wasn't an easy decision, but I had married a Canadian man and enjoyed teaching people about internet investigations.

At first, I loved the work I was doing, and it felt extremely valuable and rewarding. But even as I taught people, I often found myself feeling like I wasn't experiencing enough human connection in my work. I enjoyed the process of teaching cyber investigations, and I was good at it, but I missed actually conducting investigations. I lived in a beautiful house with my husband, I drove an expensive car, and we traveled all over the world. On paper, I should have been ecstatic. Despite it all, though, not doing investigations was leaving me feeling hollow and unfulfilled.

That's when I got the call to be an investigator on the TV show *Hunted*, a reality series created to illustrate the difficulty of living off-grid in twenty-first-century Britain. I helped track down everyday people volunteering as fugitives trying to evade capture. Working on the show made me so happy. Everything that had felt wrong suddenly felt right again. From there, everything changed. I knew I had to go back to being an investigator, even if it meant blowing up my life, which is exactly what it did. My husband and I split up, I sold the Land Rover, and I moved out of the six-bedroom house. But I had rediscovered my passion. I felt overwhelmed with a sense of responsibility to use my skills and experience to help others.

I set up my own professional investigations company, and word quickly spread. Since the launch of my business, I've had more clients and cases than I can handle, and although I'm incredibly busy, I can finally breathe again knowing I'm doing the right things for the right reasons.

Hunted has never been about the prestige, or the money, or the fame of being on TV. To me, it's about working with an incredible team. On that show, I get to work with some of the most inspiring, most intelligent people I've ever met, and I wouldn't trade it for the world. Suddenly, I have a voice to share everything I've learned after working for years on hundreds of cases, and I have the opportunity to inspire a new generation of investigators.

I knew I'd made the right decision when I unpacked all of my things in my new place after splitting with my husband. I'd had several boxes in storage that I'd never taken out in our old house. Inside one of those boxes was all of my old police gear—my training school files, my epaulets, and dozens of thank-you letters from the people I had helped. I pulled them all out, reminiscing on my time in the police service. Then, underneath the gear, something caught my eye—the teddy bear from Michael's sister.

Suddenly, I knew without a doubt that I'd made the right choice to return to investigations. I set him on my bed in my new apartment, where he continues to remind me of my decision and how I got to where I am.

RELATIONSHIPS ARE EVERYTHING

When you look at my life up to this point, it might be easy to think, "Wow, you've had a tough life. You must be angry or bitter." To that, I'd say I've been blessed. I've worked in law enforcement, and I've been a profiler, a technologist, and a professional investigator. In fact, I've led an extraordinary life, following my passions and being true to myself. However, it hasn't been easy. With every new step along my journey, I didn't really know how to begin.

As a uniformed police officer, and even as a detective, most of the time, you're guided or instructed as to what to do, either by the calls coming over the radio or by one of your supervising officers. In other words, you're usually in a somewhat reactive role. When I realized I wanted to be a private investigator, it was my first time stepping out of that structured environment. I didn't know how to go about it.

I didn't know how to start a business, I wasn't an accredited private investigator, and I didn't know for sure if I had the skills necessary to make it. I was cast adrift without any idea of where to go. I had the skills to keep myself afloat, but I had nobody to point me in the right direction. So I started reaching out to people I admired in the investigation and business fields.

I was stonewalled, every time. I couldn't even get anybody to reply to me. I wasn't asking for anything outrageous. I was just saying, "Can we have a phone call or meet for coffee?" I wanted to learn about their experiences, their downfalls, their knowledge. I wanted to learn what they had done right and wrong in building their business. I wanted—*needed*—a mentor.

The series of closed doors that slammed in my face upon reentering the industry fit perfectly with the negative reputation of private investigators that I had heard about and had, on occasion, experienced. It's a very secretive cloak-and-dagger industry that is predominantly male-driven, elitist, competitive, and quite frankly, hostile to outsiders and newcomers. Collaboration and mentorship, it seemed, were completely off the table.

Luckily, my voracious reading came in handy again at this point. I researched and studied the process for myself, which allowed me to get my private investigator (PI) license, form my own business, and create an incredible network of clients and peers. But not everybody has the time and resources to do that all on their own.

That's why I now get literally hundreds of people, many of them women, reaching out to me for advice on how to get into the investigation field. And I respond to each and every one of them because I know how it feels to be ignored by somebody you admire. It's an awful feeling to find a role model, reach out to that person, and have them ignore you.

From all the people I have spoken to, I have learned that the most common problem aspiring investigators have is that they don't know where to begin. This is a symptom of a lack of mentorship—a way for new investigators to understand the breadth of the industry and the importance of collaboration. Many people in this field won't offer mentorship unless there's something in it for them. This book is my response to what I feel is missing in our industry. I've seen investigations from the inside out. Everything I've been through, both as an investigator and as a human, has taught me that this industry needs to be more collaborative and that the people within the industry need to exhibit more compassion and empathy, especially to those who are new to the industry.

Maybe you want to get into investigations from another field, and your talents would transition really well, but you don't know exactly *how* your skills can translate. It is my view that anybody who looks for information in a directed way, regardless of the source or method, is an investigator. This, of course, includes law enforcement personnel and professional investigators like me, but it also includes journalists, people in the medical field, accountants, lawyers, and experts in the banking industry. We are all investigators, in some sense, because we are all looking for information and problem-solving all the time.

So much of becoming a world-class investigator is

dependent on your mindset rather than your job title. For example, I'll often see my daughter, who's very interested in investigations, working on a school project, and it's very much an investigation for her. She'll be verifying data based on her sources, thinking critically, and problem-solving. Most importantly, she's naturally curious and tenacious, and that mindset is fundamental to an investigator.

There's a generation of digital natives, like my daughter, out there who were born with the potential to be amazing investigators, simply as a by-product of the natural skillsets they adopt from the time they're children. However, we're at risk of letting them slip through our fingers, because in our secretive industry, we don't like to share. What differences could we make in the world if every investigator pooled their knowledge and shared the things they knew? If people cared more about their relationships with others than they did about the money, there's no telling what we could do in terms of tracking down terrorists, human traffickers, and organized crime gangs. Not only would we improve ourselves, but we'd improve the entire industry.

INVESTIGATION IS DEEPLY HUMAN WORK

I will keep saying this because it is a fundamental belief I hold: being a professional investigator is about being deeply human more than it is about the actual skills. It requires more compassion, more empathy, and more relationship skills than many other professions. In this industry, you dig deep into people's vulnerabilities. You pull back the veneer from their life and reveal the secrets they have bubbling underneath. You have to handle those vulnerabilities with great care. It is critical that you know who you are in order to exercise the level of compassion and empathy necessary for building a trusting relationship with somebody. You are a human first. Your job as an investigator is secondary.

This book goes far beyond the day-to-day tasks of being an investigator. That's why it's designed to help you zero in on who you are and where you might fit in this industry, based on what you bring from your own life and your personality traits.

We'll use the mindsets and skillsets you already possess to help you find your path to becoming a world-class investigator. From there, we'll focus on the importance of mentorship in your development, how it's often disregarded in this community, and how to fix that. Then we'll talk about how you can actually change the world through collaboration and sharing, which is a win-win for everyone.

This book not only will help you break into this industry but will also teach you how to become a world-class investigator. Anybody can work in investigations, but not everyone will be *world-class*. To be world-class necessitates that you are connected with yourself and others. It's about humility, self-discovery, passion, and working with like-minded people to help others. One of the biggest mistakes people make coming into the investigation world is that they take any job they can, disregarding their natural passions and morals for the sake of making a bit of cash. Instead, we'll walk through the process of discovering what unique personality traits you bring to investigations. What differentiates you from others in the field? What has led you here?

PART I

DISCOVERING WHO YOU ARE

CHAPTER 1

———

YOU AS A HUMAN

Your morals and ethics shape who you are as a person, which in turn shapes who you are as a professional investigator. I didn't learn what kind of investigations I *wanted* to do (let alone what I'd do well) until I came up with my personal North Star.

I learned about the personal North Star, or Polaris Point, from a book called *Prosper! How to Prepare for the Future and Create a World Worth Inheriting* by Adam Taggart and Christopher Martenson. The authors suggest that we all discover where our skills, our passion, and our knowledge intersect. The point where yours intersects is your North Star, your guiding light in the world. Figuring out your North Star is a wonderful exercise that greatly affects the work you choose to do in investigations. I'd recommend it as a prerequisite for becoming a world-class investigator. How can you know what kind of investigation work you want to do until you discover what you find fulfilling as a person?

In order to find your North Star, you must be entirely honest. Expose yourself to your own limitations, biases, and fears. That's the only way to find out what you really care about and why. Everything in your life up to this point has informed who you are as a person—everything from your religious background to whether or not you were popular in school shapes who you are and your ability to be a world-class investigator.

Sometimes we're not very skilled at something, but we believe in it wholeheartedly, and so we take the time to learn everything we can about it. Or maybe we care about something passionately, but for whatever reason, we aren't able to translate that into our investigative work.

For example, I've come to realize that I can no longer be involved in domestic violence cases, despite that being the very thing I'm most passionate about. At first, when I decided to become an investigator, I thought domestic violence cases would make up the majority of my work. I know domestic violence inside and out. I worked on countless domestic violence cases in the police force, I've been subjected to domestic violence in a marriage, and since I've moved to Canada, I've volunteered for many years on the board of directors of a women's transition house. And yet, it took only two investigations as a private investigator for me to realize that my personal morals and ethics would not allow me to work domestic violence cases. It seems counterintuitive, doesn't it? But the reason is simple. I'm so close to the subject that I find it difficult to be completely objective.

If I were purely focused on the money and getting as much work as possible, I'd take those cases. This is where it's so important to know yourself. Without my personal North Star guiding me, I would take those domestic violence investigations and potentially do them badly, causing further problems for everyone involved. Instead, I've found an outlet in my volunteer work with domestic violence that fulfills my need to work in this area without compromising myself or anyone else or getting too emotionally involved in individual cases.

You also have to recognize that the work you do might change over time, which requires some fluidity as you gain more experience and insight into who you are as a person. It can be very difficult to be this honest with yourself, but you must put in the work in this area if you are to become a world-class investigator.

It's important to get this right, because often, you won't leave your work behind at 5:00 p.m., which can be crippling if you haven't figured out who you are well enough to do the right kind of cases. Investigations can be intense, especially if you're deeply empathetic. The intensity is only exacerbated if you feel a personal connection to the case and are especially invested in its success. You have to ask yourself, "Where is the line between working an investigation and living your life?" You must set boundaries around this every single day and maintain them if you are to maintain your objectivity and professionalism.

PEOPLE CALL YOU ON THE WORST DAY OF THEIR LIVES

When I first entered police training school, one of my trainers said something to me that I'll never forget.

"When somebody calls the police, they are probably having the worst day of their life." As an investigator, whether with the police or not, a new file might be one of a dozen you're working on. But when somebody has been the victim of a crime, they feel *violated*. They feel unsafe. They're often devastated.

Sometimes, the best thing you can do for somebody is to let them know that they're being heard and that you believe them. That's what Diane did for me that was so crucial—she listened. From there, it's your job to inspire confidence that you can help people get through potentially the worst thing that's ever happened to them.

People will be coming to you from positions of great vulnerability. Help them feel safe. You might have problems in your own life, but they can't know that. You have to approach them as a figure of authority, trust, strength, and comfort. They must know that they can bare their soul to you, because even though you don't know exactly what they're going through—it could be a sudden death or a missing family member—you must approach them human to human with compassion and understanding.

These cases often don't leave you when you walk away from your desk—they stay with you. When I'm working on a case, I might not be actively investigating at any given moment, but when I'm cooking dinner, I'm thinking about it. When I'm out with my friends, it's in the back of my mind. I'm constantly questioning whether there's anything I'm missing. When you're immersed in an investigation, you don't stop thinking about it when you close your computer or leave the office. Sometimes, it doesn't even stop when you close the case.

DO THE RIGHT THING WHEN NOBODY IS WATCHING

As you solidify who you are as a person, you'll start to recognize when people ask you to do things that go against your morality. This will be a real judgment call for you. At some point in your investigative career, somebody may even offer you *a lot* of money to do something that is illegal, immoral, or both. There's a moral line for every investigator, and once you cross that line—once you compromise your integrity—there's no coming back.

There's a great saying that goes, "Integrity is doing the right thing even when nobody is watching." As an investigator, you'll be exposed to a lot of very personal information, such as financial records, private emails, and if you're surveilling people's homes, their daily habits, you'll learn the intimate details of people's lives. What you do with that information determines what kind of person you are.

COMPASSION FOR EVERYONE

First and foremost, I always advise investigators to screen the person who is hiring them. I'm very open with my clients about this. I want to know what their motivations are. Are their intentions honorable? Do I believe them? Are they trustworthy? Are they trying to hurt somebody? I don't take a file if I think I'm at risk of being in the middle of some revenge plot.

Figuring out who your client is is very important. I recently took a case for which I needed some help from a surveillance expert. Someone in my network suggested a person they knew who was highly respected. I took that recommendation and developed a professional relationship with this surveillance expert. After that case closed, he asked me to do an investigation for him.

I told him, "I'll take the case, but it will include a background check on you." He agreed to the terms. When I researched him online, I was appalled by what I found. For the purposes of confidentiality, I won't disclose exactly what he had been convicted of in his past, so I'll simply say that what I found bumped up against my morals. It made my conscience scream. I couldn't continue working for him on his case.

The circumstances put me in an incredibly uncomfortable position. What was I going to tell the person in my network who recommended him? What would I tell my client, the surveillance expert, whose online history made it impossible for me to work with him?

I decided to disclose what I'd found to the original contact in my network. I also approached the client and advised him that I was not able to take the case.

This is an example of a situation where it's important to know who you are. If you don't have yourself aligned closely to your morals and ethics, you might find yourself taking a case that you'll later regret. Both individuals responded well to my being honest with them. In fact, the surveillance expert later approached me again and asked me to help him clean up his online reputation. In this case, I left my judgment at the door and treated him as a reformed criminal. Who was I to judge him if he had worked hard to move on from his mistakes? I had a good hard look at myself in the mirror and agreed to help him.

In the end, I was able to help a person who wanted to use what he had learned in his past to help others because I treated him as a human. I had to check myself and say, "It's time for you to stop being judgmental." I've never had a case that challenged my integrity and morality so much as that one, yet through compassion, openness, and integrity, I was able to help somebody who ultimately deserved a second chance.

As a world-class investigator, your instincts will be one of your greatest tools. Trust them. At the same time, you must verify what you're seeing. When the surveillance expert approached me to take his initial case, every part of me was telling me not to take it, and I still believe I made the right choice. None of us should feel obligated to take a case that bumps up against our morals or ethics. I also believe I made the right choice later when he asked for my help fixing his reputation. I had to let go of my judgment and biases and realize he just wanted to move on with his life.

Your integrity will be tested in this industry—there's no doubt about it—but it's your job to accept or deny these cases while still maintaining respect and compassion for the people asking for your help.

A SAFE EXIT

In law enforcement, you often don't have a choice in the cases you deal with. A crime happens, a call comes in over the radio, and you respond. For the most part, you can't decide to reject a case in the same way a professional investigator can. In other words, you're not driven purely by your personal morals in law enforcement. You're driven by what you *have* to do. Your obligations are black and white.

Professional investigations are more nuanced. You'll find

that people come to you because they don't want to go to the police, for one reason or another. For example, I've worked on cases where individuals were being trafficked as a result of their not having valid immigration status. They were coerced into enslavement and abuse because going to the police may have led to deportation. So they came to me, a professional investigator.

In domestic abuse cases, you may encounter people who want to get away from an abusive situation but won't necessarily want their partner to be arrested because they feel it will negatively impact their children or because they will become homeless or financially destitute. While they don't want to be in the situation any longer, they may believe going to the police will make things worse for everybody. So they come to you, a professional investigator, looking for a safe exit. In other words, your clients' motivations will be different when they approach you as a professional investigator as opposed to law enforcement. You're usually called upon to ensure somebody's personal safety or to gather enough information to make a civil case in court. In these cases, you are not judge and jury. It is not up to you to decide whether someone's motivations are consistent with what you think they should do. You may offer advice if it is asked for, and you can ensure that your own morals and ethics hold firm, but it is not up to you to judge the motivations of your client, providing they are legal, and not intended to harm another person.

It's important to note here that being a professional investigator gives you no more rights and no more powers than any other person on the street. That often surprises people when they enter the industry. You can't suddenly start carrying a weapon and trespassing onto property just because you declare yourself an investigator.

You can find yourself in precarious positions with the law when you become a professional investigator. That's why it's so important to know exactly where the legal boundaries are, as well as your moral boundaries, since you're constantly walking the fine line between both. Law enforcement, on the other hand, is guided only by the strict letter of the law. *Usually*.

DO THE ENDS JUSTIFY THE MEANS?

In 2016, two pedophiles met on a message board known as "Child's Play" on the Dark Net. If you're not familiar with the Dark Net, it's the area of the internet that is predominantly hidden and accessible only via specific browsers or programs. It's a hotbed for child exploitation communities. These two men—one from Canada, the other from America—quickly became friends, realizing that they shared a lot of the same fantasies. Through this message board, they decided to meet up in the real world and abuse a child.

What they didn't realize, however, was that law enforcement officials who watched their every move had infiltrated their message board and knew of their whereabouts. The two were arrested and charged when they met in America, having sexually abused another child. One of the men was the leader of the entire online group, containing more than one million members. As part of his plea bargain, he agreed to give up his administrator username and password to the police, who wanted to use his account to help take down more pedophiles. There was only one problem—the online group's rules mandated that every message a member posted had an image of child abuse attached to it. This helped prove that people on the message boards weren't police officers.

Now, in most jurisdictions in the world, the law states that you cannot commit a crime to gather information on another crime. An exception is Australia, where certain police departments can obtain permission from the courts to break the law in special circumstances. In order to move the investigation forward, the entire case was handed over to a special unit, Task Force Argos, run by the Queensland police department, and the message board fell entirely under the control of the Australian police. Task Force Argos would be able to legally commit the crime of sharing child abuse images in order to gain credibility on the message group, which would allow them to capture more sexual predators of children. As a result of the infiltration and investigation of the message board and its members, by October 2017, the Australian police had gathered enough evidence to take down hundreds of the most violent and prolific sex offenders in the world, and the message forum was shut down completely.

I'm very torn about this. On one hand, their actions secured the convictions of hundreds of dangerous sexual offenders around the world. But I cannot reconcile in my mind a police officer sharing images of child sexual abuse. It's an act that I see as so unquestionably wrong that when I think of it, it makes me feel physically ill. Every time someone shares an image of an abused child, it's a further victimization of that child. Does catching those pedophiles justify the actions it took to do so? I don't know.

This is one of those rare situations when, in order to catch the worst of people, you have to become them. It's a gray area. As private citizens, professional investigators don't have the law on their side in a circumstance like that. They have to be even more careful than law enforcement. There are even more gray areas that you'll encounter in your investigations.

HOW TO HANDLE THE GRAY AREAS

In law enforcement, prejudice becomes obvious fairly quickly in a team environment. If, for example, you're in a car with your partner, and you arrest someone and make a throwaway prejudiced comment, you'll be weeded out. Not always—people do slip through the cracks—but prejudiced behavior is easily detected on a tight-knit team. Once identified, that individual will be trained, counseled, or eliminated from the the investigation team.

There are fewer checks and balances in professional investigations, however, which makes it all the more important to know yourself. We all have biases of one kind or another, and that doesn't change when you enter the investigation field. You have to know your biases well enough to reject cases that will cause an issue.

Think about how you were raised. Personally, I was raised to be very open and accepting of other people's religious beliefs and sexualities, yet I still don't fully understand other people's cultures. This isn't prejudice; it's ignorance. It's okay for you to be ignorant about something as long as you recognize your ignorance and don't allow it to degenerate into prejudice. For example, I don't know how it feels to grow up transgender. I had no exposure to a transgender person until well into adulthood. If I were to undertake an investigation centered on this issue, I would need someone to help educate me about the emotional triggers, pitfalls, and physical challenges unique to a transgender person's life. It is vital that you recognize your areas of ignorance or lack of knowledge and take steps to compensate for them through education, collaboration, and self-awareness.

Just as you'd carry out a risk assessment in police work, professional investigators must have the knowledge, skill, and forethought to conduct a *personal* risk assessment before entering into an investigation. It's an easy step to overlook, especially if, for example, you need the money, you're particularly enthusiastic about the case, or you have the opportunity to work with someone you admire. However, recognizing your own biases is necessary to determine which cases you accept, as well as the ones you should reject.

There is no place for personal vendettas or revenge in PI work. By conducting an honest personal assessment before every case—determining if it bumps up against your morals or challenges any of your biases in a way that will impact your ability to objectively do your job—you'll be more likely to check your ego at the door and conduct an honest and successful investigation.

YOUR INVESTIGATION STARTS SOONER THAN YOU THINK

Police officers go through a specific process to gather facts from both sides to solve a case, usually resulting in a criminal charge. In private investigations, you typically hear only one side of the story. You won't have the benefit of knowing whether the information you're being told is true because you can't easily verify it against the opposing side directly.

You must trust your instincts and ask the right questions. Again, this is why I screen my clients first before investigating anybody else. Have they done something wrong? Are they hiding something? Do they have an ulterior motive for coming to me and not the police? While maintaining your compassion, you can even explicitly ask them their motivations. Some of the questions I ask my new clients include the following:

- Why are you hiring me, specifically, as opposed to someone else?
- What else have you done already to solve this problem?
- What are you going to do with the information I give to you?
- Why haven't you reported the situation to the police?

I don't ask people these questions to trick them or catch them off guard. I ask them because I want to know who they are and what their motivations are. I want to know if I'm going into a situation that might put me in personal danger. I have no interest in being used to help someone exact revenge against another person or ruin another person's life or reputation, and I don't recommend you take that kind of work either.

A good way to ensure that you and your client have aligned expectations and that the information you are being provided is accurate, honest, and complete is to have your clients sign a client engagement agreement. Essentially, this document will outline what the client has told you, what their expectations are, and a statement reiterating that they are telling the truth. If you subsequently discover you have been lied to about anything, it can negate your professional relationship, and you can decide whether to continue with the investigation.

Your investigation doesn't start when your client signs that agreement or when you get your retainer. It starts the moment you meet your potential client for the first time. I make a point of asking questions and signing the engagement agreement in face-to-face meetings with people. Usually, I will not take cases over the phone or over email unless a client is in a location or situation that makes it difficult to meet face-to-face.

At the very least, I want to talk over Skype. Why? So when I talk to a person, I can look into their eyes, hear the inflections in their voice, and determine if they're telling the truth. Are they emotional? Are they vengeful? Are they psychotic? People telegraph their thoughts through their facial expressions. The human brain is not separate from the body. You need to see your client's face and, ideally, body language to analyze where they are mentally. This ability to read other people's emotions is what makes us human. It is something machines cannot do, and it's an important factor in establishing facts at all stages of an investigation.

HUMANS INVESTIGATING HUMANS

For years now, my Sunday routine has looked like this: I get out of bed, I wander around in my pajamas, I make a giant pot of coffee, and I spend my day watching TED Talks. This relaxing routine helps me replenish my mind and my body. One Sunday recently, I watched a talk by a techno-sociologist named Zeynep Tufekci, called "Machine Intelligence Makes Human Morals More Important." Tufekci explained the differences between artificial intelligence and human intelligence. One line in her talk really resonated with me. She said, "We cannot outsource our responsibilities to machines. We must hold on even tighter to human values and human ethics."

This is exactly how I view artificial intelligence as it relates to the professional investigation field. Machine learning, which is a computer's ability to learn by itself, is my greatest fear for the future. We are entering an era when humans may potentially no longer have control over what machines can learn. Intelligent machines are programmed with a baseline algorithm, and from there, they can continue to learn independently. It is my fear that, at some point, we may lose control of what they are able to teach themselves because their ability to learn will be exponentially greater than our ability to control them. If this happens, we'll be at risk of losing our humanity.

I believe that all investigations are grounded in human traits such as compassion, integrity, and empathy. Perhaps a robot can read body language or a computer can ingest huge amounts of data and produce an amazing analysis, but they can't reason. They can't think critically in a way that determines how emotions and feelings motivate a person's behavior.

Our focus should always be on the human aspect of the investigation because we interact with the world as human beings. However, artificial intelligence will become more intertwined with investigations as time goes on. This is referred to as augmented intelligence. For example, geospatial profiling is a vital part of many online investigations. Geospatial intelligence refers to automated programs that can ingest raw data based on geographic boundaries and find patterns, anomalies, or specific events or individuals within that data. With API (application programming interface) inputs from various social media platforms, such as Facebook, Twitter, and

Instagram, we can find posts made at a specific location by a specific individual within a designated time frame, or a combination of these parameters with less defined boundaries. Without advancements in technology, we wouldn't have access to these tools that save time or provide previously unavailable information.

As crimes become more complex, so too will the tools we use to solve them. We can't be afraid of technology. We need to understand its place in the industry and use it for collaboration and understanding. If you don't understand technology, you must have the confidence to reach out to someone who can help you. I see a lot of older investigators who are life smart but technology naïve. I also see many younger people coming into the field who are technology smart but life naïve. The ideal solution (and one of my many reasons for writing this book) is to help digital natives connect with older, more experienced investigators. New investigators and younger digital natives need someone to help guide them through the nuances of the industry (how, as an investigator, to not end up in jail, for example), while older, more experienced investigators would benefit from the knowledge of the digital natives and those who understand today's rapidly evolving technology.

There are lots of former police officers who have been in the force for twenty years or more and want to get into professional investigations as a second career. They know the nuances of the work. They've seen everything. They've done everything. They know the law inside and out, but they can't work their way around the internet. They don't know what the social media landscape is like, what apps people are using, or what technology is currently available to monitor digital communications. At some point, you will need to collaborate with other people to assist you in areas where you do not have the knowledge or skills that you need. (We'll talk more about collaboration in Chapters 5 and 6.)

Data is neutral. Humans, who are capable of reason and discernment, are necessary to interpret that data based on other known factors that change the meaning or motive. If we lose our humanity—meaning we hand over all of our tasks to machines that will crunch numbers and come to conclusions without critical human analysis—we'll lose our industry.

Crimes are committed by humans. There are still significant interpersonal skills and psychological factors that determine the success or failure of an investigation. We are still humans investigating humans. Almost every case comes down to motivation. Why did the person do what they did? A machine might be able to figure out who did what and when, but will it know why? It can process data, but it has no context for the data, let alone moral conviction or intuition. Only you, as a human, can answer the most vital questions in an investigation.

WE ARE ALL FLAWED

Being a world-class investigator is not only about what you know, what you're good at, what your experience is, and what you want to do. It's about looking at yourself and knowing who you are on a deep level.

It's also not enough to recognize your current morals and ethics. You have to recognize *where those values came from*. What influences did you receive from your friends and family as you grew up that formed your sense of self? What are your prejudices? How are your political and sociological views going to skew your abilities as an investigator? These are hard questions to answer, but they'll bring you closer to the realization that you won't be perfectly objective about *any* investigation you encounter.

There are people you will encounter in this industry who will be willing to bend the truth or the law for their advantage. Don't let that person be you. The most important thing you can do to remove temptation or resist that behavior is to remain aligned with where your personal North Star sits. As important as changing yourself is, it is also vital to recognize that something needs to be changed in the first place. You don't know where your blind spots are until you look for them. In other words, you can't make any progress without first calling your attention to your own biases.

When I was a brand-new police officer, still under supervision, my very first duty was to give out traffic tickets. One of my first stops was an elderly man driving in the bus lane.

"Are you aware that this is a bus lane?" I asked.

"Yes," he said, "and I'm very sorry."

"I'm going to have to write you a ticket."

"Yes, I understand."

People are often upset when they receive a ticket, but the look on his face was despondent. I could tell there was something else going on. I asked him if he was okay.

He looked down and shook his head. "Not really," he said. "My wife has cancer, and I just got a call from the hospital. They told me to get there as fast as I could to say goodbye to her. That's why I'm in the bus lane."

I've never been able to fully forgive myself for what I did next. I gave that man the ticket. I did not treat him as a human being. I treated him as a number. I didn't have the moral courage to say, "You know what? I'll get in my car and escort you to the hospital. You're not in an emotional state to drive, but we need to get you to your wife to say goodbye, so let's at least make sure you get there safely." That's what a compassionate investigator—a world-class investigator—would have done.

The people you interact with aren't a number or a box for you to check. Nor are they just a paycheck or an exciting case to talk about with your friends and peers. They are human beings. When you interact with people in this profession, you are a big part of their day, and how you behave affects each person's life. I don't have many regrets in life, but giving that man a ticket is something I wish I could take back. However, it has shaped who I am. That experience has guided many of my decisions since that day, and anytime I question my morality, objectivity, or empathy, I think back to that man, and the answer becomes clear.

We all make mistakes. We have biases and prejudices that impede our objectivity. We aren't machines—we're flawed—but those flaws are what make us human. If you recognize your flaws and do the best you can to minimize them, you'll be more prepared to know who you are as a human being and as an investigator.

TO DO BEFORE MOVING ON

- Create your North Star.
- Identify your biases.
- Determine the boundaries of your morals and ethics.

CHAPTER 2

YOU AS AN INVESTIGATOR

Now that you have a better understanding of who you are as a human being, the next step is figuring out how to use your skills to become a world-class investigator. You might be proficient in many areas, but the most common question at this stage is, "Where do I start?"

Every day I get emails and messages from people asking me how to break into the investigations field. I typically respond to their inquiry with a question of my own—a question I want you to consider throughout the course of this chapter—"Where do you want to focus?"

FINDING YOUR FOCUS

Professional investigations are a multifaceted industry. There are so many specializations that you can get lost trying to become proficient in them all. As you continue to hone in on who you are as an investigator, you'll want to start eliminating the niches of the industry that don't intrigue you and focusing on those that do. That's what I had to do after I took on a transformative domestic violence case.

THE CASE THAT CHANGED MY FOCUS

A woman came to me alleging that her abusive ex-husband was stalking her. They'd been separated for some time, yet he followed her everywhere she went—their children's school, the nanny's, and other after-school activities. She told me he'd even put tracking software on her computer and on the children's cell phones. There were harassing emails. Threats. A fake Facebook profile. The list went on. With every grievance against her ex-husband, another red flag raised in my mind. And not for the reasons you might think.

First, when I interviewed her, her story was very convincing. Too convincing, in fact, to the point that it almost seemed scripted. Second, when people lie, they often provide too much detail. They'll tell you unnecessary information in an effort to convince you what they're saying is true. The woman's story put big checkmarks in both of those categories for me, so my suspicions were raised to high alert.

After she finished with her overly detailed story, I asked for her permission to look at her computer and the children's devices to check for any tracking software. When I examined the headers of the harassing emails, it was immediately apparent that they had been sent from a computer using the same IP address as her own. I suspected that the messages were likely sent from within her home through a fake email account she'd created. There was also no evidence of tracking software on any of the devices she'd claimed were being tracked.

Just to be sure—because you must always be sure—I returned the following day, packaged everything up, and sent it for forensic examination to get a definitive answer as to whether the devices were being remotely monitored. When the analysis came back, it turned out there actually was tracking software on the devices. However, the software had been put on the devices *after my visit*, not before. I concluded that the complainant knew computer forensics would need to find something for her story to survive, so she installed the software after my visit but before the forensic examination to help corroborate her story.

Unfortunately for her, I had thoroughly tested my instincts and my theory. I reinterviewed her, methodically laying out the evidence that suggested she might be lying. It didn't take long for her to throw in the towel. She confessed to fabricating her story, admitting that she was desperate to remove the children from their violent father, so she had hired me to help bolster her case for full custody of the children. The outcome was devastating for everyone involved.

HOW TO NARROW YOUR FOCUS

Working on this case completely changed my focus. From that day on, I knew I didn't want to be used to another person's advantage. This case wasn't the first time someone had used a professional investigator to do their bidding, and it wouldn't be the last. But it would be the last time someone used *me* for this purpose.

I've always been passionate about helping victims of abuse, but I couldn't help this woman if I was investigating a fake trail based on fabricated evidence. On that day, I decided I would stay away from domestic violence and abuse cases that had any connection to child custody. This was not an easy choice for me. I am extremely passionate about helping victims of abuse. But I am so passionate that I know I find it difficult to be entirely objective, and I'm susceptible to being manipulated. I decided there and then that I'd leave the police or other investigators to handle those types of cases in the future.

Sometimes you have to experience the negative side of investigations to discover where you want to focus your efforts. I'd always had a general idea of my ambitions related to investigations, but my experience with that particular client forced me to focus more intently on other areas that I was equally passionate about.

YOU MAY NOT BECOME THE INVESTIGATOR YOU THOUGHT YOU WOULD

Focus is what establishes your trajectory in your work. It can be based on your innate morals, ethics, and interests, but it can also be influenced by life events, like it was for me with the domestic violence case. In other words, your focus will be directly related to who you are as a person.

The biggest lesson I learned from that abuse case was not to get stuck on one facet of investigations. Maintain your fluidity, and recognize that you're going to evolve as time goes on. Even if the focus you've chosen is something you believe in deeply—it aligns with your morals, your ethics, and life experiences—it doesn't necessarily mean it's the right fit for you. Domestic violence cases ticked every box for me and aligned perfectly with my North Star. They focused on my need to protect women and children. Yet, they still turned out to be a bad fit because of my biases and emotions around the subject.

Take my word. It's jarring to realize that you may not become the investigator you thought you would. To be used as a tool to *hurt* others, the very thing I wanted to prevent, was intolerable for me. That case made me realize I needed a more thorough examination of my own path. I had to be adaptable.

WHY IS FOCUS IMPORTANT?

As an investigator, you have the freedom and opportunity to go in any direction you choose. You can focus on cyber investigations, corporate fraud, surveillance—you're virtually unrestricted in the kind of investigations you want to pursue. So do your research.

Today, with rapidly evolving technology, you cannot master everything. Instead, you should try to build expertise in one or two narrow niches. Ultimately, focus is necessary for getting started and moving forward with investigations. Having focus in a specific area or niche, especially when it relates to your passions and interests, will provide you with the excitement and drive that you need to advance in your career as a professional investigator. The more cases you solve, the better your reputation will be, the more people you'll help, and the more fulfilled you'll feel.

However, picking a niche you love doesn't necessarily mean you will be good at it. For example, I absolutely love surveillance, but I don't have a knack for facial recognition. As I've grown and developed my skillsets as an investigator, I've run into that situation multiple times. I find a niche that I think would be interesting, but I can't pursue it because I know my real talents will thrive elsewhere. Often, as we try to develop our skills in one area, we discover previously unknown talents or interests that take us in another direction entirely.

One such example involves my daughter, Stephanie. When she was little, she was such a tomboy, but she didn't have one specific interest. I threw her into many different sports—gymnastics, swimming, soccer, and hockey, to name a few—but nothing stuck. We went through *everything*.

Then one day, she tried out to be a cheerleader. I thought there was no way my Stephanie, the tomboy, would ever be interested in being a cheerleader. But to my surprise, it was exactly what she'd been looking for. Through trial and error, she'd found the thing she loved, even though it wound up being something entirely contrary to her personality and the things she thought she was interested in up to that point.

WHAT BROADER CATEGORIES OF INVESTIGATION SHOULD YOU BE AWARE OF?

Figuring out your focus will likely be a real test of personal fortitude. You might stumble into it like Stephanie did, or you might have to struggle through it like I did with the domestic violence case. Either way, it's going to be a roller-coaster ride. You will face disappointments. However, there's always room for improvement and discovery in investigations. As you move toward your focus and continue to learn more about the industry, you'll come into contact with four very broad categories of investigations, which are all worth exploring.

FINANCE

I always tell people, "If you want to be an investigator, but you don't like dealing with people, investigate financial crime." Financial crime encompasses a broad spectrum of crimes to investigate, such as money laundering, identity theft, cryptocurrency fraud, and blackmail. Due to the extensive automated components in financial and organized crime, it is one of the areas of investigation with less human interaction and more technical analysis.

You'll encounter a lot of organized crime in this area, which is often run like a corporation. The fraudulent enterprises frequently headquarter in areas you may not be familiar with, such as Russia and the Middle East. At the top of the "corporation" is the kingpin, or "CEO." These organized groups gather information, often by way of hacking or theft, then use either fear, coercion, or enticement to scam their victims via phone calls, email, or text. They are able to reach millions of people every day, using bots or other automated tools.

Their risk of detection is low, and even if the criminals are caught, their punishment is usually relatively light. I'll be honest, financial fraud can be hard to investigate. You'll be investigating automated tools, bots, and networks that are intentionally difficult to understand.

For example, there's a whole industry predicated on fraudulent insurance claims. A common scam in this racket is for a person to fake a car accident in order to make a personal injury claim. It can be difficult for insurance companies to disprove personal injuries, so they typically pay out, unless they can prove that the claimant is fabricating their story.

Although challenging, financial investigations are great for avid problem-solvers. Every day, you're forced to think outside the box, learn something new, narrow down the facts, and reassess all the possibilities, while simultaneously following multiple digital threads and online footprints.

OFFENSES AGAINST PERSONS

Investigations in this category range from online harassment, such as social media stalking, to pedophilia. With the digital world at our fingertips, committing an "offense against a person" has never been easier, and yet solving such a case has never been harder. With videos, photographs, applications, social media, and an increasing lack of online privacy, online abuse and harassment have become prevalent.

One distressing by-product of our increasingly digital lives is something referred to as revenge porn. The term was coined after several cases surfaced in which people had created fake social media accounts and posted nude images of their "enemies" online for the world to see. These fake or photoshopped pictures were typically accompanied by slanderous comments to discredit the victim, successfully ruining their reputation, career, relationships, and in some cases, their entire life.

Of course, there are still many cases of abuse and harassment that happen face-to-face, but there is a growing need for skilled investigators in the digital realm.

CORPORATE

Several types of investigations fall under the corporate umbrella, but perhaps the crime that's trending the most today is ransomware on corporate computers. In order to use ransomware to their advantage, a criminal often needs to accompany it with social engineering. One method of attack is to figure out who the most vulnerable target is in a large corporation and to obtain their personal information.

Once they've identified a victim, the criminal will make acquaintance with the person, whether online or in person. Then, after they've broken down barrier after barrier, the victim will reveal something scandalous or threatening, such as a nude photograph, a password, or some confidential information. From there, the criminal will infect all the corporate computers with a ransomware program that threatens the victim, saying, "If you don't pay up, I'll reveal the photo/information."

Blackmail using ransomware commonly takes place on an even larger scale, often by securing compromising emails that could negatively affect an entire company rather than an individual. Typically, the company will pay up to save themselves. Even after paying the ransom, the information might still be leaked. Either way, the company is put in a very precarious situation.

Another example of a corporate crime I dealt with was an internal personnel issue within a large, multinational corporation. One of the company's employees, a Muslim woman who'd grown up in a non-Muslim country, was transferred to a Muslim region because of her ability to speak a specific language. In the country she transferred to, some of her behavior that was not strictly Muslim—especially as an independent, career-focused woman—was frowned upon. It didn't take long for the harassment to begin.

The harassing messages were sent using a fake email address within the company's internal email system. Because every employee was a suspect, including the IT department, it made sense for the company to bring in someone like me to be their professional investigator. In this situation, you have to work closely with the company's senior management team and have a keen eye for pattern analysis as well as some technical knowledge to determine when, where, and how the emails were sent and where they were routed.

Recently, I worked on an investigation where a large company had a concern regarding online radicalization of one of their employees. This person showed signs of becoming disenfranchised at work, as well as in their personal life, and began escaping into a world of radicalization—in this case, ISIS. In partnership with a forensic psychologist, I conducted a workplace violence threat assessment, which helped to identify the patterns of escalation and threats to the organization. The individual was eventually fired after threatening to assault another staff member.

As you can see from my examples, corporate investigations tend to involve a much more hands-on approach. Complex cases such as these require creativity, mental dexterity, and often quite a lot of technical knowledge. To investigate corporate crimes, you must have the strength and confidence to handle everything from harassment and cyberbullying to extortion and high-level corruption, all while maintaining excellent judgment, a sharp mind, and clear vision for pattern-solving.

Because of the complexity and the unique skillset and experience they require, corporate investigations often come with the biggest monetary advantage for investigators. Why? Most individuals will have a limited budget or desire for hiring a professional investigator. Corporations, on the other hand, have a public image and a responsibility to the individuals whose private information they hold, so it's in the company's best interest to pay you when that image or information is threatened.

LARGE-SCALE

Though corporate crimes can certainly become large-scale, this category of investigation will most often relate to international or multijurisdictional crimes involving cults, organized crime, terrorist activities, and human trafficking.

I've dealt with a number of investigations involving cults, whether religious, spiritual, financial, or political in nature. Most of the time, cult organizations could be likened to pyramid schemes—a business model that is predicated on every participant recruiting more members.

Terrorism, on the other hand, can range from radicalization of individuals online—which I've predominantly worked on—to singular events, such as the Boston Marathon bombing or the 7/7 bombings in England.

Both cults and terrorist organizations usually represent sophisticated, organized crime, meaning you will more than likely have to conduct your investigations with a team. There will be no "going solo" in this category. Multiple minds must come together to fight the types of injustice you'll find with investigations in this category.

In addition to having a team, you must also have a clear understanding of the ideologies that inform these groups' plans. We tend to be suspicious or dismissive of stories related to brainwashing, mind control, or hypnosis, but with cults and terrorist groups, their use of psychological manipulation is finely tuned.

Large-scale crime can be extraordinarily difficult to wrap your mind around, and there's often an immense amount of hard work that goes into accomplishing even the smallest of goals. This category is not for the faint of heart or anyone with a short attention span.

BREAKING DOWN THE CATEGORIES

Regardless of the investigation types you choose to pursue, there will be several elements that they all have in common.

PSYCHOLOGY

The most common element is the need for psychological analysis, which starts with the motivations of your client. *What is their state of mind? What is their reason for hiring you? What are their expectations?*

If you're delving into things like cults, coercive control, domestic abuse, child sexual abuse, and human trafficking, you'll have to do some research and figure out how best to investigate them. *How do they recruit people? How do they brainwash their victims?*

At the start of every investigation, you'll have three entities you need to focus on—the person hiring you, the person or group you're investigating, and yourself.

We all like to think that we're not susceptible to social engineering and manipulation, but intelligent, self-aware people like you and me get caught up in pyramid schemes, cults, and domestic abuse situations all the time. *What motivates us? Is it greed? Fear? Boredom? Or does it have more to do with our desire for purpose and belonging?*

TECHNOLOGY

Another commonality in most investigation types is the involvement of technology. *What are the technological elements of the situation you're investigating? Are the criminals using the internet to recruit people? How are they using technology to commit their crime(s)? How can you use technological tools or digital data to assist you in your investigation?*

INTERPERSONAL WORK

Almost every type of investigation involves advanced interpersonal skills on your part. *How well do you communicate with your client? How will you build trust? How will you ask questions, use body language, and use other communication skills to get to the truth? How well can you relate to the person or the entity you're investigating?*

USING THE CATEGORIES TO MOVE FORWARD

Being a professional investigator, no matter what area you choose to work in, will require you to have working knowledge of psychology and technology and to have excellent interpersonal skills to facilitate relationship building.

To find your niche, start by taking stock of your current knowledge base or interests within these common elements. Maybe you're entering the investigation field after years of service in another industry. What information can you bring with you from your prior experience? What passions have you developed over the years? Why do you want to be an investigator? Asking yourself these questions will help you narrow down your options and choose an area of specialism that's the best fit for your talents and passions.

TURNING YOUR KNOWLEDGE AND PASSIONS INTO EXPERTISE

Let's say you love fashion, and it's part of your everyday life. In college, you had a successful blog that you used to sell clothing. You have an intimate understanding of the fashion world, everything from where certain brands are manufactured to the season's hottest styles. In addition to your wealth of knowledge about fashion, you're a curious and tenacious person, which is why you want to be an investigator. How can you have the best of both worlds? How can your knowledge of the fashion industry and passion for clothing be incorporated into your career as an investigator?

First, state the facts. You know an awful lot about fashion, you know where clothing products come from, and you know how to source cheap clothes.

Then ask yourself some questions that may point to possible criminality linked to the fashion industry. *How can you identify the supply chain? How do you determine whether these clothes are counterfeit or not? If dealing with counterfeit clothes, how do you find out where they're being manufactured? Do they use child labor?*

The answers to these questions will help you build your interests into your investigation's expertise. Perhaps you love the fashion industry but decide you wish to focus on eradicating child labor. This passion might very well drive you on to investigating modern slavery in the clothing manufacturing industry.

Although most people wouldn't automatically connect fashion to human trafficking or modern slavery, the link is somewhat obvious upon further examination. Any expertise you have can be utilized in investigations. It's just a matter of recognizing your skills and determining how they can be applied to your prospective investigation niche.

For example, let's say you've had a career in banking, so you have extensive knowledge about how the financial sector works. You may even have an expansive network of colleagues in the industry. If you've worked for a multi-national bank or a company that deals with anything from Western Union and credit transfers, then you already have knowledge about fraud. You know how money is moved around the world. You know which people are considered to be politically exposed. You know where the global hot spots are for financial crime and money laundering. In other words, when you transfer to the investigation field, you'll already have a wealth of working knowledge about finances that you can apply.

You might be thinking, "The financial industry doesn't interest me anymore. There's a reason I no longer want to work in banking."

Even if you're no longer interested in your former industry, you can still make good use of the skills, expertise, and network you've cultivated over the years. You may go on to become an expert in organized crime, organ trafficking, gun trafficking, or drug trafficking. Because you have intimate knowledge of the financial flow around the globe, you know how money moves around. You could apply your skills to the Dark Web or digital currencies, using your expertise to investigate how money moves around in illegal networks. With investigations, there are countless ways to utilize your skills from any industry, not just finance, without being stuck in an uninspiring job or a career that does not satisfy you at all.

FINDING YOUR PURPOSE POINT

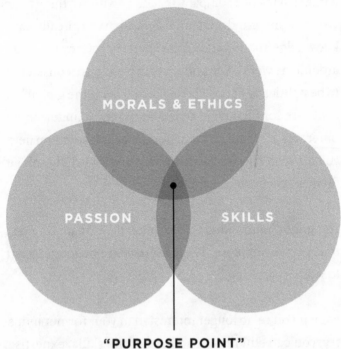

MORALS & ETHICS

PASSION

SKILLS

"PURPOSE POINT"

FINAL TAKEAWAYS ON FOCUS

Knowing who you are as a person—where your knowledge, skills, morals, values, and ethics align—is the basis for becoming a world-class investigator. You need to take a good hard look at yourself and figure out what you bring to the table in this industry. Recognize that you have biases. Accept that you have fears. Identify the gaps in your knowledge and experience.

Knowing what kind of investigator you want to be will be your foundation in this journey. At this stage, you should feel as if you've had a bit of a revelation, as though you've discovered something about yourself that you didn't realize before. Maybe you've recognized a new way your knowledge can be applied to investigations. Regardless of how intense your self-analysis has been in this chapter, you should, at the very least, feel closer to discovering your focus as an investigator.

In the next chapter, we will take that focus and teach you how to apply it to the industry. After the introspection of this chapter, it's now time to start looking outward. Once you have discovered your "purpose point," how do you move forward as an investigator? Where do you fit within this industry? What mindsets do you need to adopt to become a world-class investigator?

TO DO BEFORE MOVING ON

- Find your purpose point where your morals, ethics, passion, and skills overlap.
- Based on your purpose point, brainstorm possible areas of investigation focus.
- Remind yourself that your purpose point may change over time.

PART II

THE MAKING OF AN INVESTIGATOR

CHAPTER 3

THE WORLD-CLASS INVESTIGATOR'S MINDSET

When people envision life as an investigator, they often picture what they've seen in the movies. They think of the chase scenes, hackers, and spying into homes with binoculars. Without a doubt, you'll be in some situations where you feel like you're in an action film. It's important to remember, however, that being a professional investigator is more about having the right mindset and skillset than it is about being the next James Bond. Investigators solve problems. Investigators evaluate sources and data. Investigators find the truth by examining facts and eliminating bias and speculation.

THE INVESTIGATOR'S MENTALITY

Mindset starts with the belief that you have the ability to be a world-class investigator. Regardless of the investigation type you choose, you will be entering people's lives and building deep, trusting relationships with them. You will be the one to guide them through a difficult period of their life. In such emotionally taxing interactions, your skills and your ability to perform in the physical aspects of the job, such as sliding across the hoods of cars, are not nearly as important as how you approach the work from a mental standpoint.

Being an investigator is a position of great responsibility. It's about connecting with people, whether it's with your client or with other people in your network. It's about problem-solving—figuring out where all of the pieces fit. It's about critical thinking and the evaluation of sources and data. It's about finding the truth, no matter how difficult it is. It's about maintaining your morality and integrity, without cutting corners, even if you believe you can get away with it or it will lead you to something valuable.

A common theme in the personality traits of world-class investigators is relentless curiosity. With every case, you embark on a quest for answers that doesn't stop until you solve the case. And almost every case is solvable. You're investigating something that happened, meaning somebody did it, which in turn means that there is most likely evidence somewhere. If it was intentional, what was their motivation? If it was unintentional, was it an impulsive act or an accident?

It's an all-consuming, intoxicating, amazing pursuit. As I work through every investigation, my mind is continually building a mental spiderweb, joining every piece of information—a cognitive link chart. There is layer upon layer of information to collate, analyze, and eliminate until I've narrowed it down to a most likely scenario—a hypothesis. Even when you have a hypothesis, you can never stop asking questions and keeping your mind wide open.

You must pursue every line of inquiry until there's nothing left to pursue. Then, once you reach a dead end, you go on to the next one. If you work hard enough, you'll eventually uncover the truth, whether it takes weeks, months, or even years. You and your client must make a collective decision to determine how long the investigation will continue, which is often based on their available funds, and whether that timeline is realistic for what the client hopes to learn from the investigation.

I have known several investigators, myself included, who have ended up devoting some of their own time just to satiate their curiosity or to conclude a case when the money runs out. Ultimately, if something has happened, the truth is out there somewhere.

THE NEXT GENERATION

If you are a parent, you know certain things about your children. Likewise, if you don't have kids, rest assured that your parents know more about you than you think. It's one of our jobs as parents to recognize these innate talents or abilities and help our kids hone them.

As my daughter, Stephanie, grew older, I focused on developing her character and resilience, and equipping her for the real world. I never focused too much on her grades in school. Instead, I focused on her achievements and failures, and when she failed, we'd discuss why. My goal with this method of parenting was to teach her that when you're faced with a difficult situation, there's almost always an opportunity for a creative solution. Failure isn't something to be ashamed of or to feel guilty about, but rather a chance to learn something new or train your brain to think differently.

That's the same kind of mindset I try to foster in the future world-class investigators I mentor. Investigation is about being open-minded, asking "what if" questions, eliminating misinformation, gathering facts, corroboration, evaluation, and collaboration. The right mindset for a world-class investigator is a combination of all these elements, along with a constant desire to find the truth.

COLLABORATION

Though computers have certainly made finding information easier, it is still invaluable to have a personal connection to experts in your niche. It's great to have associates all around the globe whom you can go to for help, especially if you have an inquiry in a location you're not familiar with. It's also valuable to develop and maintain relationships with professionals of cultures, lifestyles, or languages that are different from your own.

If you are hired for a case that involves Sikhism, for example, but you are not familiar with the religion, culture, or languages involved, then being able to call someone who is can be invaluable. It's particularly useful to have connections in other countries, whether it's with journalists, forensic scientists, or psychologists. You never know where your investigation may lead you. Fortunately, technology allows you to collaborate with just about anybody. You have the potential to build up an amazing community.

As an investigator, we must do more than just collect what we find. Being observant is vital, but it's not the same as problem-solving through creativity, tenacity, and perseverance. We must seek out information, which takes more direction than observation, and sometimes that means reaching into our network to collaborate.

DEVELOPING A SKILLSET

As you develop your investigative skillset, you should start with what you already have at your disposal. What past experiences did you enjoy? What experiences did you dislike? What are your passions? You should have narrowed these down in the previous chapter.

Now you need to figure out how you can use what you've already learned to improve your investigations. Remember, you gain insight and knowledge by moving forward and learning along the way. Thinking up new ideas is helpful, but if you're not testing them or applying them, then they will never come to fruition, and you won't develop expertise. There are millions of new ideas in the world, but so many people do not follow through with their implementation because the work is too arduous or their initial enthusiasm wanes over time.

If you've found yourself in a situation where you need to develop your skillset further or don't have many skills to begin with, then it would be a good idea to try out some different types of work or find a volunteer position. Volunteering is an efficient way to develop skills that will be transferable to the investigations field.

Every industry has its own language. For example, governments in all countries are notorious for using convoluted nomenclature. Likewise, the financial industry utilizes so many confusing acronyms—PEP, AML, SFPF—that you'll think you fell in alphabet soup trying to decipher it all. Each field related to investigations has its own terminology, acronyms, and ways of communicating.

By volunteering for different positions and opportunities, you can broaden your knowledge of how different areas of the investigations world operate. Taking the steps to learn the language of the industry you would like a career in will not go unnoticed by those who might hire you. You can integrate into any industry—not just investigations—more easily if you've done your homework and can show that you're familiar with the language, culture, and mechanics of that industry.

Say you want to get in to the police service, but you don't have the right qualifications or experience. You could start by volunteering with a police agency as a community safety officer or a special constable. That way, you can build up your base of knowledge while still helping your community. Likewise, you'll make connections in a network of people that might include potential mentors or influencers.

There are many ways to build transferrable skills, not just

through volunteer work. As you build up your experience, you may need to take on roles or jobs you don't ultimately want. Look at it as a learning experience; you're taking the steps to show the industry that you're serious. Plus, the more environments you familiarize yourself with, the more people you'll get to know. Skills are important, but people are more important.

At the core of an investigator's mentality is resourcefulness. If you don't have the relationships or skillsets necessary to thrive in your chosen field, then it's in your interest to explore every avenue through which you can gain those advantages. You might have to sacrifice your time, or even your ego, to gain experience, but a world-class investigator wouldn't have it any other way.

BUILDING A BRAND

At this stage of your career, you must have an open mind and be willing to take on new opportunities. Developing your skillset and becoming an expert in a certain niche will set you apart from the competition and help you build a brand for yourself. Having a personal brand and being relatable to a certain audience will help you build a following, secure clients, and promote your success.

What does building your brand look like? In this day and age, it's a good idea to become conversant in the use of social media and create a professional image. You want to be taken seriously. Make your personal accounts private, and keep your public accounts professional. If a client searches for your name online—which is likely—you want them to see only quality results.

At the same time, it's vital to be honest and genuine in your approach to your online presence. People cannot get behind a persona that lacks authenticity. Clients don't want to work with someone they feel they know very little about. If you try to be someone you're not, you will eventually fail.

Building a brand might seem like an egocentric process, but it's a critical step in informing your potential clients about who you are. Consider how your audience can best receive your content and learn about your mission. Then you can start the process of expanding your network through your online presence.

PRIVATE INDUSTRIES VS. THE GOVERNMENT

As you refine your purpose point and use it to choose an investigation niche, you must consider the difference between private work and government work.

With private industries—especially large-scale corporations—it is in their interest to remove you quickly if you don't deliver excellent service, even if it means they pay more for an alternative.

The world of government contracts is a slower-moving machine, which affords the possibility for greater job security. If you can create a positive track record with at least one government contract, you're likely to obtain more contracts in the future. You become a known entity and therefore a lower risk.

Government contracts can also be worth a lot of money, so they're ultracompetitive. You have to be skilled, fast, *and* competitively priced to obtain a government contract. Likewise, investigators with previous government experience, such as police officers, often receive preferential consideration. As a new investigator, if you don't recognize your relative lack of experience, you might spend precious time chasing government contracts that you aren't likely to win.

Instead, you can work with more experienced investigators as a subcontractor. For example, a few years ago, the government of a small country in Asia put out a request for proposals to help them deal with their growing human trafficking problem. Someone in my network wanted the contract, but he couldn't fulfill all of the requirements himself, so he partnered with other experts to create a group bid on the contract. One subcontractor would develop tracking software for shipping containers, one person would monitor the ports, another investigator would search cargo types, and so on. They won the contract.

Most of the subcontracted experts were less experienced than the main investigator, but by bidding jointly with him, they gave themselves a chance to establish their own positive reputation with the government. It was an opportunity they wouldn't have had access to on their own.

SEEK OPPORTUNITIES TO LEARN

As a professional investigator, you cannot expect information to be simply thrown at you. You must continue to be curious, which means constantly seeking out ways to learn and receive new information. Education is key to becoming a world-class investigator. Learn where to find high-quality training programs from reputable, proven sources. Join industry associations, which, quite often, will offer suggestions for training. However, recognize when people have biased recommendations. For example, when you join certain industry associations, often the people on the board of directors are the ones offering the training.

Do your background research so you aren't taken advantage of. Then find out what works best for you. In your investigation niche, do you need to receive an accreditation, a certain qualification, or a certificate? What will add the most value to your resume? Based on what kind of investigator you want to be, you can decide on where to train and to what level.

Maybe classes aren't for you. Another route you can take is seeking out experts in your area of interest. Ask yourself, "Who do I want to be in ten years?" and try to find someone who embodies what you want for yourself in the future. Reach out to them. See if they're interested in mentoring you. *What training do they have? What skills do they have? How did they get to where they are today? What is it about them that you admire? How do their traits fit in with your personality?*

If all else fails, you can turn to the internet. Developing a skillset and building your network does not have to be expensive. Most of the tools and connections you need today are available at the click of a button. Just remember to always validate your resources. Social networks, such as LinkedIn, provide fantastic resources and articles to help you connect with potential mentors. You can use YouTube tutorials to help train yourself in some skills quite effectively. You may also consider looking into online message boards and forums, where you can speak to and collaborate with others trying to find the same information you are seeking.

No matter what path you take to improve yourself as an investigator, your mindset always revolves around learning. Expanding your network, improving your skillset, and seeking out mentors are all learning processes. Likewise, as you meet more people, you begin to see your own work from a new perspective. Your next goal is finding someone to develop the most learning-focused relationship possible—a mentor.

TO DO BEFORE MOVING ON

- Determine the areas in which you need to improve the most.
- Research opportunities to gain experience, even if it's volunteer work.
- Continually reapply this learning mindset as we move forward in the book.

CHAPTER 4

MENTORSHIP

THE ULTIMATE COLLABORATION

Doug came to me the way the best mentors do—by accident.

Ten years ago, the company I worked for focused on internet investigation and education. We traveled around the world teaching and training people on how to use the internet as an investigative research tool. Though our ideas were great, the company's business model wasn't. The senior management were excellent practitioners but not great at business leadership. The company suffered as a result.

Over lunch one day, I was chatting with an associate from a different industry, telling him about our issues. He suggested I talk with a businessman he knew, a man named

Doug who ran a construction company. I was skeptical. How could a construction company, a completely unrelated field, help us grow our internet investigations training business? But their company was booming, so I thought it was worth a try.

Doug's office was in a warehouse, where we were bombarded by a million noises all at once. At first glance, he was not the kind of guy I would have ever considered asking for advice. He was brash, outspoken, and had zero filters. My team and I walked in dressed in suits. He was in jeans and a plaid shirt.

Aside from my associate who recommended him, there was no connection between Doug and my team. He knew nothing of our business, and we knew nothing of his. Yet by the time we left that first meeting, the fire of my curiosity was burning bright. Despite my finding the man opinionated and having nothing in common with him, something about his straightforward manner intrigued me. He worked through problems differently than anyone I'd ever met. I couldn't quite put my finger on why, but I knew I wanted to learn from him.

Two weeks later, we met again. At first, I found the meeting frustrating as he questioned and challenged our decision-making and business practices, but I reminded myself to be open-minded, as I believe everyone has something to teach us. Then, like a light switch, something clicked. During that second meeting, I realized why he seemed to solve problems differently. Doug had severe dyslexia, which led him to see problems in a nonlinear way by working through things backwards. He automatically reverse-engineered *everything*. Suddenly, I was aware of his genius.

I continued to schedule weekly meetings with him, eager to learn more and more. The CEO of my company eventually stopped coming to the meetings, as the disparity between their opinions became too great to overcome. However, despite our CEO's reticence, my new accidental mentor became more invested in our company, eventually becoming a 10 percent shareholder.

As my connection with Doug grew, so did our company. He was astute enough to recognize that I'd hit a glass ceiling within our company, and Doug wanted me moved to a position of greater leadership, stating that he would relinquish his 10 percent if I wasn't made president of the company. I was in shock. So was the CEO. However, we couldn't deny the truth. The company would not reach its full potential without a major change. It just so happened that change was me.

We took a chance and changed things up. While the CEO kept his position, I took over as president, just as Doug (forcefully) advised. Under the advice of my unlikely mentor, I broke through the glass ceiling and shifted the psychology, focus, and success of our company.

Mentorship is essential for expanding your knowledge and depth of understanding. A good mentor like Doug will help you see your situation from an outsider's perspective. You won't always like what they have to say, but if they're a good mentor, they'll tell you what you *need* to hear, not what you *want* to hear. Keep an open mind. You never know who will hand you the keys to your success. They might be someone you already know, or they could be a brash stranger wearing jeans in a warehouse.

Remember, you don't seek out a mentor because you want to stay the same. A mentor is not meant to help you stay in your comfort zone. A mentor will help you grow, expand the way you think, and gain a different perspective, and they will guide you and care about your progression. Your growth will be uncomfortable, and your mentor's beliefs may challenge some of your preconceived ideas, but that's the point of mentorship—to challenge you to learn.

To be honest, I haven't liked most of my mentors. At first. If they're good, mentors will reflect your deficiencies back to you. They hold up a big mirror and show you your shortfalls, not to hurt your feelings but in order to make you better. For a perfectionist like me, that's always been a hard process to embrace. It wasn't until I advanced in the investigations industry that I truly appreciated all my mentors had done, even if they frustrated me at the time.

REFLECTING YOUR WEAKNESSES BACK TO YOU

I loved my team when I was a uniformed police officer. We all shared a close bond because we were often put in life-or-death situations together. We spent as much time together outside of work as we did on shift. We laughed and cried together and fought side-by-side on the streets every day. However, one day, I received a letter from a superior officer, Inspector Andy Williams, informing me that I was being moved to a new team with immediate effect.

I was devastated. My team meant everything to me; they were like my second family. I took the letter informing me of the transfer, marched into Inspector Williams's office, and angrily voiced my frustrations. Despite my demeanor, he calmly and diplomatically explained why he'd chosen to move me.

"It's not about numbers," he said. "I've watched your performance. I'd like to help you develop as a police officer. I think you've got great potential, but you're at a point where you've gone as far as you can go on your current team."

It took me a long time to admit it, but Andy was right. Even with our rocky start, for the five years following that meeting, Andy took me under his wing. His unlikely mentorship with me culminated in my final case on the police force—the investigation where Diane and I found Michael's missing body.

Despite being five months pregnant, my determination did not wane one bit during the investigation. In my mind, I was still invincible. But Andy knew me by then, and he realized, as my mentor, that the best approach was not simply to tell me what to do or what not to do. I would have only responded with more tenacity and fire. His job was to lead, support, and help me learn and develop as an investigator.

Diane, Andy, and I searched for Michael's missing body through pitch-black nights, scouring forests, hills, and secluded ravines. When we came across dangerous situations, Andy would place his hand on my shoulder and say, "Are you sure you should be walking on train tracks?" or, "Is climbing over that barbed wire fence at six months pregnant a good idea?" He challenged me—without ridiculing or belittling me—to confront my own stubbornness.

He forced me to ask myself some incredibly difficult questions. Even if my tenacity would help us with the investigation, what price was I willing to pay for success? How could I rationalize jeopardizing our case, endangering myself, and most importantly, putting my unborn baby at risk to find Michael's body?

With all the paternal care of a true mentor, Andy urged me to step back and reassess my choices. Though I wanted to dislike him, and it took time for me to realize he'd be another profoundly influential mentor in my life, Inspector Williams saw in me what I could not see in myself—a world-class investigator just waiting to burst into the world.

A part of me knew back then, as we trekked along the nighttime train tracks—lit by nothing but the silver light of the moon—that I needed Andy and Diane, no matter how independent I was. I didn't always heed their advice (hence my being on train tracks in the middle of the night at six months pregnant), but their guidance compelled me to see things from a new perspective.

I walked through the darkness in many ways on that case, the same way I did when I first met Diane. With her kindness and compassion on one side of me, Andy's paternal guidance on the other, and my unborn baby, Stephanie, within me, I knew I did not walk alone.

YOU CAN'T OUTSOURCE YOUR HUMANITY TO TECHNOLOGY

A society as technologically advanced as ours necessitates that investigators understand themselves and other people more fully. More and more investigation work is becoming automated. It's your duty as a world-class investigator to maintain the thread of humanity through your investigations, especially when you rely heavily on technology.

You can't be a twenty-first-century investigator without using technology in one way or another, whether it's cell phone analysis or open-source intelligence gathering. Whatever part of the job you're doing, you will use technology at some point.

What does more pervasive technology use mean? It means it's more important than ever to surround yourself with other people—fellow humans whom you can sit and talk to face-to-face. It's easier than ever to disregard real relationships. You need people around you who can guide you in ways technology can't and who remind you why your work as an investigator is important.

Automation is great for condensing time and solving analytical cases faster. However, automation also means isolation—we can get so immersed in the virtual world that we forget about the real world. Great investigators cannot work in isolation. You must maintain human connection and collaboration, and a great way to maintain it is by engaging in a process-oriented mentorship.

EXPERIENTIAL LEARNING

Mentorship is a means to maintaining your humanity through collaboration. That's what mentorship is, after all—a collaboration with someone who advises you through uncertainty. It's about taking someone on a journey—both mentor and mentee—to help each bridge their passion with their curiosity to foster a desire to see the world change.

I recommend finding a mentor who focuses on process-oriented mentorship. In other words, you want someone who values experiential learning, which means you both learn by doing, as opposed to learning from a textbook.

You can get your "textbook learning" from the courses you take or certifications you get related to investigations. This type of learning will be great for mastering a specific skill, such as open-source intelligence gathering or reading body language. In those circumstances, textbook-type learning is a good way to efficiently absorb information.

Mentorship is something different altogether. It has a strong emotional element to it. Your mentor's teachings, as opposed to textbook learning, should be more focused on assimilating the investigation industry through experiential learning. They should give you things you can't get from a textbook, such as accountability and encouragement, all while they continue the learning process themselves.

It's very similar to a parental relationship. Having a mentor is almost like having a parent there to guide you through your high school years or college. You have the freedom to grow and learn on your own, but they are willing to step in and provide guidance when you need it. It's a relatively hands-off type of relationship. A large part of your mentor's function will be keeping you accountable.

They can oversee the type and relevance of the training courses you're taking, guide you in volunteering to learn more skills, and maintain a critical eye over how you're doing with your work. They provide an objective person for you to sit down with and discuss how you're doing overall—this is the emotional element of your relation-ship. You'll share with them what courses you took and what you learned. A good mentor will listen to you and counter with tough questions. For example, if you just told them you took a surveillance course, they might say, "Where do you think it will take you? How do the skills you learned in that course fit into the big picture of everything you're doing as an investigator? How are you going to measure your return on investment from that training?"

By asking tough questions, your mentor will keep you moving forward down the right path. They have a very broad strategic overview of your work. When you're focused on the nuts and bolts of investigation—trying to develop practical skills and generate more business— they'll help guide you back to humanity.

Sometimes your mentor will be nothing more than an emotional outlet. Other times, they'll be the worst schoolteacher you've ever had. They'll tell you that everything you do is terrible and that you've wasted your time. They'll let you know when you're driven by ego, you're not taking advice, or you're too focused on money.

Your mentor will keep you on track. They're not in your life to provide validation. They offer encouragement and accountability to help you focus on your tactical and strategic goals. As you go through the pain of growth and development as a world-class investigator, a good mentor will guide you.

Sometimes their guidance will feel terrible. Sometimes it will feel amazing. When the years pass by, and your mentor becomes your peer, you will look back and realize that even when you disliked what your mentor reflected

back to you, you needed their guidance. From that realization, you will know when it's time for you to become
a mentor yourself.

FINDING A MENTOR

Your first step toward finding a mentor is reaching out
to your inner circle and letting them help you. There's
a common saying that goes, "We are the average of the
five people we spend the most time with." If you've surrounded yourself with people who make you better (and
vice versa), they will likely know other people who can
help guide you in the right direction.

Next, go back and think about the categories from Chapter 2—financial crimes, offenses against people, corporate
crimes, and large-scale investigations. Figure out which
category you most want to work within, and then define
your interests and passions. Look at your skillset too.
Which of your skills in that area are underdeveloped?
What are your strengths? The answers to those questions
will help narrow your focus and lead you to a mentor who
can help you improve your weak spots.

Then take a moment to look back on your life. Can you
recall anyone who became a mentor to you, whether by
accident or on purpose? What were they like? What personality traits did they exhibit that made you better? Use

those characteristics from your former mentor—even if they were infuriating—as a guide to find a new one.

The ideal mentor for each person will be different. A mentor might be great for one investigator, but awful for you. Likewise, your ideal mentor might be the person you don't *want* to work with, but they are the person you *need* to work with. Someone who challenges you to the point that you dislike them might be exactly what you need to become a world-class investigator.

If you don't have access to anyone who fits the characteristics you need in a mentor, then consider taking part in a mentorship program. Through such a program, you can gain exposure to several experts in your designated field while also building a network of collaborators.

One of the most important things to remember is that you can have more than one mentor. Specific skillsets and certain categories of investigations might require different mentors. For example, when I needed to learn more about artificial intelligence (AI), I knew my mentor at the time didn't have any knowledge in that field. I had to go out and find an AI expert to mentor me on the subject. In another investigation, I needed to help someone who was trapped in a cult. I knew very little about coercive control, so I reached out to a cult specialist in my network who helped me solve the case. We still work together to this day.

Or maybe you'd prefer to invest your time with a jack-of-all-trades. Whether you choose multiple mentors or just one, the point of your relationship is to get out of your comfort zone and broaden your skillset and your mindset. With an open mind and a genuine willingness to learn and grow, who knows what could happen? You might even teach your mentor a thing or two in the process.

RESULTS OF A SUCCESSFUL MENTORSHIP

Once you've found a mentor and have started working with them, you'll have a lot to look forward to. Having a mentor can be a big confidence boost. You now have someone in your corner who knows and understands the pathway to success. It's also an excellent form of encouragement to have your mentor listening to you and holding you accountable, while being a cheerleader, coach, and business advisor all rolled into one.

At the same time, having a mentor presents challenges for you. Your mentor, over time, will learn your weaknesses and your strengths. Of course, they'll be there to guide you through your struggles, but they'll also present you with questions that may lead you to inward and outward conflict. Be prepared for this; it won't be easy.

Mentorship is a very selfless endeavor, but it can be mutually beneficial. You want a mentor who is there to learn just like you are. Together, you can grow and form a bond that will become important to both of you. There may be times of conflict and resentment. You'll likely butt heads with your mentor from time to time, particularly as you grow in confidence and strength, but don't let that discourage you.

A successful mentorship is measured by the growth of your mutual experience. There is no proper definition of success or failure—only how you and your mentor define it. Choose your goals and allow your mentor to help you achieve them. Experience the results together, regardless of the pitfalls in between.

Then, when it's time to let go, a great mentor will know when to step away. When you've hit that glass ceiling, a great mentor will allow you to break through, even if you don't take them with you. No mentorship is lifelong. Your mentor will impact your life, of course, but eventually— just like teaching a child to ride a bicycle—they'll have to let go of the handlebars and allow you to go forward without them.

Once you move beyond your mentor relationship, it's time to focus on collaboration—taking what you've learned and sharing it for the benefit of others rather than only learning beneath the expertise of an individual mentor.

TO DO BEFORE MOVING ON

- Look back and identify your previous mentors, even if you didn't realize they were mentors at the time.
- Determine what you liked and disliked about them.
- Seek out mentors who have strengths where you need improvement.

PART III

JOINING TOGETHER TO CHANGE THE WORLD

CHAPTER 5

COLLABORATION AGAINST ALL ODDS

When I first joined the police, I was in my early twenties. The technology we are all dependent on these days wasn't around. People didn't carry smartphones, Facebook didn't exist, and Twitter was still several years away. Our only sources of information were proprietary police systems and information collected from the streets. So our actionable intelligence came from databases, the UK Police National Computer, and the intranet. In short, it was a different time.

Six years after I joined the force, having taken a role as a field intelligence officer, I made my first arrest as a direct result of internet-sourced intelligence. The crime was armed robbery, and the only clue was a photograph of the suspect's clothing. It was my job to search our databases for the criminal's distinctive jacket. I looked everywhere, but I found nothing matching his description. I knew there had to be *something*—the jacket was so unique. So I took to the internet.

At this point, Facebook was in its infancy, so there weren't nearly as many people on it as there are today. However, the armed robbery suspect was young, so I thought he might be on social media somewhere. Sure enough, within hours, I came across a photograph of some local youths. One of them was wearing the jacket.

Despite its unique logo and design, I knew I needed to do further research, just to make sure I had the right person. In the background of the photograph was a street. I identified where that street was within our division. Then I searched our local police systems and did a cross-reference to confirm that the youth wearing the jacket in the Facebook picture matched the photograph of the person who committed the armed robbery. It was a match.

With the help of leading-edge technology, I had solved a serious crime, and inadvertently discovered a passion that would soon become an integral part of my career.

Over the years, the police service evolved with the times. We moved from using the internet as a commercial tool to using it as a collaboration tool and communication forum. Email became more prevalent, and we joined social networks.

People willingly put more and more information on the internet. From Facebook to Instagram to Snapchat, the changes have been exponential. We went from sharing our information purposefully to divulging information routinely and automatically. Social media has become such an integral part of our lives that it now raises suspicion when someone *doesn't* have an online presence.

HOW TECHNOLOGY LEADS TO COLLABORATION

Today, I have investigations based in the Middle East, Europe, Canada, the United States, Asia, Central America, and the UK. And guess what? I'm doing all of those investigations from my laptop, wherever I happen to be at the time. Thanks to technology, I collaborate seamlessly with experts in those regions when I need someone to do work on the ground, which allows me to undertake investigations all over the world. Encryption, artificial intelligence, and blockchain technology keep my communications and data secure and instantly accessible.

When I first started working with my last company, Toddington International (TII), the availability of technology allowed us to offer a full spectrum of services. For example, we could undertake forensic examinations in-house if a case required it.

However, as technology's reach has grown, our areas of expertise have shrunk. It's no longer possible to be an expert in everything. There is too much to know and massive amounts of data to process.

As these changes took place, we felt the effects at TII. Our focus was predominantly on training, so anything that didn't fit the bill eventually became outsourced. The first service to go was forensic examinations, and it wasn't long before investigations followed.

Over the course of a few short years, we went from being a full-service digital investigations firm to a specialized training company. As the transition took place, I became more and more unhappy. I missed investigations, and although I enjoyed the interaction of training (and got great reviews), I wasn't passionate about it. I started to dread going to work.

Then one morning, out of the blue, I got the call to be an intelligence expert on *Hunted*, and just like that, I was thrown back into investigations. It was exhilarating; I suddenly felt alive again. I knew, without a doubt, that doing investigations was my calling. I tried to integrate investigations back into TII, but our reputation and client base was firmly fixed in training. So, I made one of the most difficult decisions of my life. I left. I followed my heart back into investigations, seeking out mentors and collaborators to help guide me. Although it wasn't the easy path, I came out on the other side excited and ready to face the next challenge in my life.

Because of the complexities that technology added to the investigation field, the company I had helped build for ten years had become something I could no longer be a part of. As crimes have become more complex, so too have the investigations that seek to solve them. Rather than spread yourself too thin to meet clients' needs across all categories of investigation, it's more important than ever to find your niche. From there, it's time to build a network of collaborators.

TECHNOLOGY EQUALS COMPLEXITY

Though I left my job at TII, that company's evolution provides the perfect example of how technology has created a more complex industry. It's extremely difficult to operate without a niche these days. Once we realized we could outsource the things that didn't fit entirely within our areas of interest and expertise, we did so. Our focus narrowed to training, and those who didn't want to narrow with it—like me—eventually had to move on.

It seems counterintuitive that the ever-expanding technologies available to investigators, and the greater opportunities they offer, would necessitate that you limit your specialties. However, because technology has created areas of investigation that require incredible depth of understanding, you're better off finding a collaborator to fill the gaps in your knowledge. The alternative is spending your valuable time learning every investigative niche and its associated technology.

If someone asks you what your job is, your answer can no longer be, "I'm an investigator," without adding, "specializing in..." It's just not possible in the information age to know everything about every aspect of the industry. You may need to explore several areas of investigation before you discover your specialty. Then you have to devote your time to developing your knowledge and skills until you are truly an expert.

That's not to say you can't have a business running different types of investigations. It just means you're an expert in one or two things, and either you employ other investigators with different areas of expertise, or you develop a trusted network of collaborators and industry professionals to outsource the parts of investigations that don't fit within your capabilities.

That being said, you should not use collaboration as an

excuse for ignorance. A world-class investigator does not say, "Well, I don't know anything about that type of investigation, so I'll just outsource it and forget about it." That's not what collaboration is about. It's okay to admit that you don't know something and ask for help, but from there, it's up to you to learn from your collaborators so you can work together more effectively. Eventually, you'll understand what is and isn't possible in their area of expertise. You might even teach them something in the process too. Collaboration is all about sharing knowledge. By constantly learning, you can make yourself more valuable to your clients and future collaborators who need your help.

As companies grow to accommodate new technology, our professional networks must do the same. That doesn't mean we must know everything about all facets of investigation. It simply means collaboration is more vital than ever to survive in this constantly changing world.

COLLABORATION IS EVERYTHING

I have seen many small investigation firms trying to keep every part of their investigations in-house, which can limit their ability to help their clients, as well as limiting the growth of the investigative community. You must collaborate with other investigators. A world-class investigator recognizes the parts of an investigation they can do on their own and which parts would be more effectively solved by another expert in their network.

Despite the growing need for collaboration, everyone I've spoken to as I've researched this book reports that although communication is easier than ever before, collaboration has, in fact, diminished. It's unfortunate because, although we live in a world where we share more private information than we ever did in the past, investigators are more protective of their resources, techniques, and networks than ever. Technology has given us so many ways of connecting, yet many people just isolate themselves even more.

We've created our own competition.

There's a battle between privacy and convenience playing out across the internet, and we no longer know where to draw the line. If you want to install an app, you have to provide your email address, your contacts, and sometimes even access to your camera or microphone. If you want to join a network or a group, you have to give up access to your personal information. There's always a payoff.

The same dynamic is playing out in investigations right now. You usually won't get something for nothing. If you want to grow your reputation and your business, you must collaborate, which means you must give as much as you want to take. It's the nature of the world. Information is currency.

I COLLABORATED MYSELF OUT OF THE CASE

I recently took on a complex blackmail case. It was a situation involving organized crime within a medium-sized corporation. An employee developed an ongoing relationship with someone through the internet. Unbeknownst to the employee, this new internet acquaintance was a criminal. Their relationship allowed the criminal to manipulate technical and private information out of the employee, including passwords for important company documents. The criminal then used that information to install ransomware, which allowed them to hack into the corporate system and blackmail the company with sensitive information.

I couldn't solve this case without collaboration with other investigators. The company originally came to me because they knew I had a good reputation, but I recognized their need for experts in hacking and financial crimes. Although I have some knowledge of those categories of investigation, they aren't my specialties. However, I do know plenty of investigators in my network who have extensive experience working on cases like this one, so I contacted them to enlist their help.

As the investigation went on and I recruited more people for the project, my role became smaller and smaller. Rather than let my ego get in the way, I allowed my collaborators to take the reins of the investigation. To me, investigations aren't about gaining glory or being Wonder Woman; they're about solving the case. And the best way for me to do that was to collaborate.

If I had isolated myself and tried to solve a case as big as that one alone, it may still be unsolved to this day. I would've sat at my computer trying to train myself on areas of expertise I had little knowledge about. I would have let that company down—tarnishing my reputation—but perhaps more importantly, I would have let myself down.

A great investigator knows his or her capabilities and limitations. They know when others can do the job better, and they're happy to share the workload, and possibly learn something along the way. Why? Because investigation isn't about winning; it's about helping.

THE NARCISSISTIC DOWNSIDE OF TECHNOLOGY

As niches narrow and technology grows, we will only become more protective of the information we hold—even more so than we already are. This does not refer to client and case information, of course, but to methodology, case studies, successes and failures, and work that could create collaboration and new networking opportunities. You may ask, "Shouldn't technology increase openness and collaboration?" In a perfect world, yes, but we're still human—we still feel a natural compulsion toward competition, even when it's not helpful.

The wealth of information we have available at our fingertips at any moment represents a power unlike any we've ever known. With that power typically comes a monetary or career-advancing reward. However, many of us choose to use information to better ourselves rather than to better others. It's part of our egocentric nature.

The climate we were raised in also affects how competitive we are, especially millennials, who have grown up in a socially dynamic and technologically advanced environment.

Our self-absorption only exacerbates our isolation. With technology, too, both our attention span and our need to talk face-to-face have decreased. Our communication skills are in decline. If you go into a restaurant or sit on the train, you'll see fewer and fewer people talking to one another. Instead, our eyes have slowly shifted downward, focused on the content of our screens.

With the prevalence of social media, we're also seeing

a rise in idealism and the need to project perfection. There's a certain air of happiness and success we all try to exude online, even though we may not be that way in reality. You might think you know someone based on their online presence, but until you meet them offline, you don't really know them at all.

Our online personas have given us the ability to design a more perfect version of ourselves, which has created impossible standards to strive for in real life. As we constantly compare our lives with others we see online, our expectations of ourselves become increasingly more difficult to reach.

We've also become more financially and idealistically motivated. I see many investigators take great care to reach their goals, yet when someone asks them how they did it, they don't want to say. Why keep it a secret? They want ownership of that success story, and they don't want to share it with anyone else. Because we live our lives online, every success and failure is amplified. We feel as if everyone is watching and judging us all the time. Conversely, we'd rather watch someone struggle to the top like we did than pull them up using the advice we wish we would've had.

Suddenly, we live in a world that doesn't have time for anything other than work. Work, work, work, *work*. You don't have time to communicate, sit and have a coffee, or stand in the office and chat, because if you want that promotion, or if you want that better lifestyle, you have to work harder than everybody else. That means putting in more hours, fulfilling more contracts, and completing more investigations—the faster the better—even if you lose your human connections in the process.

Instead, you need to step away from this narcissistic mindset and focus on collaboration. Not even competitiveness is an excuse for isolation. In fact, the more you collaborate, the better both you and your collaborator will be at your work. You and the people you collaborate with in your network will be able to take on more diverse cases than the "lone wolves" in the industry, which will make your services more desirable and expand your scope and your reach. In the end, being an open collaborator—one who is willing to give and receive help from your network—will bring you success faster than even the most competitive of solo investigators or insular companies.

HOW ORGANIZED CRIME GROUPS COMMUNICATE

As our tendency to keep to ourselves grows, criminals increasingly recognize it as a weakness. And they are correct. Organized crime—from fraud to terrorism—makes as big an impact as it does because criminals do in abundance that which investigators often resist—they communicate.

Large-scale terrorist groups such as ISIS use technology to collaborate very effectively by adopting a group mentality, albeit fragmented, which keeps their overall ideology and efforts unified. That's not to say that ISIS or any form of criminal group is *in any way better than the people investigating them*—not at all. They are simply using the same technology that is available to investigators to carry out specific goals, even if their motivations are horrific. They work toward a common purpose, and they do not allow that purpose to become sidelined by competitiveness or ego.

WHAT'S YOUR GREATER PURPOSE?

I once worked on a case where numerous employees at a global corporation were victims of fraud, but the local police in each jurisdiction did not take the complaints seriously. Each incident was so small—a minor breach here and there—that the officers that took the reports didn't feel it warranted a full-scale investigation. They were too busy working on higher-profile cases that would improve their status in the community and among their peers. Meanwhile, the criminals behind the fraud were able to use this uncollaborative culture to continue collecting huge volumes of information about the company's proprietary secrets, including emails and passwords.

Here's where the communication problems came in: each employee being exploited in the company assumed they were the only one who'd been targeted. The management and staff of each location didn't talk to each other to help stave off more attacks, so the attacks kept happening, and the police kept receiving report after report and also didn't communicate with each other.

When I eventually stepped in and investigated the incidents, I realized that there were more than thirty victims of the same crime spread across the entire company. Had they talked to one another and gone to the police *together* as a company, or had the police joined the dots of these relatively minor offenses sooner, the crime would've been recognized for what it was—a full-on attack on their infrastructure and their intellectual property.

This example is indicative of the growing lack of collaboration in our society. Unfortunately, in many cases, criminals and terrorist networks are better collaborators than the "good guys." They often have more time and more resources, are more motivated, and feel they have less to lose. Of course, they are also not as constrained by morals and ethics, or by the law. However, even within these groups, there is often a "moral code" of sorts, as well as a hierarchy they adhere to.

Meanwhile, an investigator's colleagues might support

him, but they can't help him pay his mortgage. Though the investigator is surrounded by people who *should* have his back, his industry is not behind him but often competing against him, guarding their secrets so they can gain an advantage and take care of themselves first. This type of isolation and atmosphere of suspicion and paranoia leads to demotivation, demoralization, extreme pressure, and ultimately disillusionment. In that way, the terrorist groups and criminal organizations have a huge advantage over the investigators.

ROBERT PICKTON AND THE DEADLY EGOS

Robert Pickton was a serial killer who was convicted of killing twenty-six women in Canada in the late twentieth century, although in his prison-cell confession, he stated that the actual number of victims was forty-nine. Robert's brother owned a pig farm in British Columbia, which Robert used to his advantage. He would pick up prostitutes and other vulnerable women, then take them back to the pig farm where he'd physically and sexually abuse them. He then murdered them and fed their remains to the pigs.

Pickton was eventually caught in 2002, but the investigation was flawed from the start. There was enough evidence to catch Pickton sooner, but the information was scattered across different law enforcement agencies, and investigators did not collaborate. When the police found evidence linking Pickton to the murders, high-ranking officials took to political posturing rather than collaboration. When other people didn't agree with their conclusions, the investigation stalled among the in-fighting and chest-thumping.

People let their egos, their political agendas, and their selfishness keep them from solving the case as quickly as possible. People lost their jobs over this case, but more importantly, many women unnecessarily lost their lives. Would things have been different if the officials in charge of investigating the case had been more willing to collaborate?

WHAT TO TAKE AWAY FROM THE CRIMINALS

At the end of the day, the only thing stopping us from using collaboration to fight criminals and terrorists is our inability to let go of the competition and replace it with a focus on helping others. Working with the same single-minded focus as organized criminals—to communicate, organize, and mobilize toward a future we believe in—could reduce their impact dramatically. It is within our reach.

We have the technology. We have the channels of communication and the methodologies secure enough to protect our identities. We have ways of sharing and collaborating. Now more than ever, with these large-scale criminal operations indiscriminately targeting innocent people around the world, we need to come together and use collaboration to our benefit. We must eliminate the "keep your head down and do your own work" mentality.

There is a growing gap in the way we communicate and collaborate. The time has come for us to start working together as an industry. The incoming generation is comprised of digital natives; they're used to communicating through technology. Consider the possibility that they have something to teach other generations about effective communication in the digital age.

They also have greater access to mentorship, which in turn may make them more open to utilizing it. However, as we move into a more automated world, we're at risk of losing the unique generational crossover we have right now. As digital natives and the digitally naïve both operate in the workforce at full strength, we are facing an unprecedented opportunity to collaborate and mentor each other in ways that have never really been possible before. The older generation should be teaching the younger generation the tools of the trade—the things you can't learn in a textbook—and the younger generation should be teaching their older counterparts how to use emerging technologies. But we're in danger of letting this opportunity slip through our fingers, because we're too secretive to ask for help or to share what we know.

We must keep in mind that everybody knows something, but no one knows everything.

We need to change our mindset. We need to stop being so suspicious of each other. We need to realize we're at a critical juncture in our industry. If old and new investigators worked together to create a unique and powerful force, we could crush organized crime and put a huge dent in terrorism, human trafficking, and other growing global crime epidemics.

If we don't collaborate now, we may lose our opportunity to merge great investigative experience with great technological expertise.

TO DO BEFORE MOVING ON

- Check your ego and ask for help. Don't become a lone wolf.
- Recognize that your goal is to solve the case, not strive for glory.
- Use technology to connect rather than allowing it to isolate you.

CHAPTER 6

BUILDING YOUR NETWORK

In the outskirts of London, more than 450 cats have been dismembered since 2014. Though some people think a group of killers is behind this atrocity, the cats have all been similarly dismembered, leading investigators to believe that these heinous crimes have been committed by a single individual, dubbed the Croydon Cat Killer.

When cats first began going missing and then showing up dead, people thought they were being killed by foxes or other animals. However, as the Croydon Cat Killer developed his craft, he started beheading felines and placing their heads on school gates as public evidence of his crimes. He would leave the rest of the cat's dismembered body on the porch of the house where the cat had lived.

As more time passed, the scenes grew more graphic and brutal. Meanwhile, the police didn't appear to be doing much about the issue, leading to a public petition containing over thirty thousand signatures, imploring them to step up the investigation. Complicating the matter was that the crimes had taken place across several different jurisdictions, so one police jurisdiction might have two dismembered cats—not especially shocking by itself. However, two jurisdictions over, there might be three, and a few more miles from that, there would be five. The numbers grew and grew, but the collaboration was lacking between the different police forces. They didn't realize how big the issue was until each jurisdiction had several dead cats on their hands.

In fact, the first people to make the connections were veterinarians and regional animal welfare organizations. They calculated the number of cat killings across a certain geographical area and came to the realization that there was a serious problem, so they started to investigate. Once they compiled their information, the vets took it to the police, but again, the police didn't take the issue very seriously, initially.

In this case, the police lumped the data and the source together, causing them to dismiss both. It was a big mistake. The vets had good information because they were invested in the care of people's pets and people trusted them. They had insight into a field in which the police had relatively little knowledge. If they had recognized their own lack of knowledge and taken the help from an external source at the outset, or more importantly, if they had separated the data from the source altogether, the police might not be where they are with the case today.

Now, four years later, more than 450 cats are dead and the killer has evolved. He's moved on to rabbits and other outdoor pets. As his murderous skills transfer to other animals, there is a real fear that he may evolve to killing a human.

The Croydon Cat Killer, eventually, could become a serial killer of humans.

In this case, the police forces involved were guilty of two forms of collaboration failure. Not only did they fail to share information with other police agencies, but they also failed to recognize their knowledge gaps and accept help from external sources that had vital information to move the investigation forward.

EVALUATE DATA AND ITS SOURCES SEPARATELY

When you don't collaborate, you might as well be a machine. In the case of the Croydon Cat Killer, the people in charge of the investigation didn't separate the veterinarians from the data they provided. Just because the sources weren't trained investigators didn't mean they couldn't be valuable to the case—quite the opposite, in fact. And it may have been the case that the veterinarians had an abundance of information that the police did not possess because people report deceased pets to animal welfare organizations rather than the police in many cases.

As an investigator, you can analyze data all day long, but if you don't look for external sources of data or visit the actual crime scenes and see the evidence for yourself, you won't fully grasp the emotion of what happened. There is so much information that can't be communicated through raw data alone. The police ended up being severely disadvantaged in this case, and the Croydon Cat Killer remains at-large.

The job of an investigator is to carefully scrutinize information and ascertain the facts. As you do so, you need to evaluate the data and the sources it comes from separately.

During tragic events, many people want to help. Though help may be needed, wanted, and appreciated, there is such a thing as too much information. When it comes from sources that are unverifiable or uncorroborated, it can lead to groupthink and mob mentality, which ultimately can lead to people jumping to the wrong conclusions.

When a tragedy happens, people instinctively push blame—even hatred—onto someone, *anyone*, to try to find reasons or justification for the event. This is a form of confirmation bias—the tendency to see only what you want to see, as opposed to what is really there. When we are motivated to solve a case, we have a tendency to latch onto the first piece of information we find that supports our hypothesis. We might refuse to let it go, even in the face of opposing evidence. Evaluating the source of the information separately from the data itself provides some mitigation from the dangers of confirmation bias and maintains the objectivity of the investigation.

Receiving information from unknown or untested sources can be crucial, but it should also be done carefully. Two major public investigations perfectly illustrate this point—the Boston Marathon bombing and the Vancouver Stanley Cup riot. Following both of these incidents, the media and police intentionally shared specific details with the public to seek help in solving the cases. However, the request for public assistance had vastly different results in each case.

THE BOSTON MARATHON BOMBING

The Boston Marathon is a huge annual event, drawing tens of thousands of spectators every year. At the 2013 race, on April 15, among the crowds of spectators were two terrorists preparing to detonate a bomb at the event. In the hours leading up to the detonation and subsequent carnage, the terrorists were captured on the cell phones and cameras of spectators hundreds of times as they mingled with the crowd. In the aftermath of the explosion, people continued to whip out their phones, photographing and videoing the scene.

Within hours, police had released descriptions of the suspect's clothing and backpack to the media and asked for the public's help in identifying them. Immediately, users on the popular website, Reddit, mobilized and formed a discussion group to gather information using the police description to try to identify the perpetrators. Anyone carrying a package or bag that fit the police description, or anyone seemingly of the right ethnicity, instantly became a suspect as people jumped on those tiny details and made assumptions. As the frenzy grew, and more photographs and video footage was shared in the group, a dangerous case of groupthink began to emerge until, victorious, the group named their prime suspect based on their "investigation." There was only one problem. They identified the wrong person, an individual named Sunil Tripathi.

This man and his family immediately began receiving death threats, as members of the message forum posted as much personal information about Sunil and his family online as they could find. The police came forward to tell the public to leave this man alone—he was not responsible for the Boston Marathon bombing—but it was too late. On April 23, 2013, the body of Sunil Tripathi was found floating in the Seekonk River in Rhode Island. The cause of death was eventually deemed to be suicide.

Because the groups of people, both online and off, didn't have the experience and knowledge of trained investigators, and they were not sharing their information directly with the police (rather, they were forming opinions without any guidance, experience, and only a little knowledge), they were blinded by their confirmation bias, and their behaviors led to a witch hunt for an innocent man.

The terrorists were correctly identified in the end through excellent investigation work. While beneficial to an extent, public involvement in a large case can create more turmoil than help because everyone wants to be right. However, the solicitation of public information can work out in favor of the investigation, like it did in the case of the Vancouver Stanley Cup riot.

THE VANCOUVER STANLEY CUP RIOT

In the aftermath of the Vancouver Stanley Cup riot, the police asked the public for any information they had about those who were present or involved in the crimes and public disorder. People responded with zeal, sending in tens of thousands of images, hours of video, and countless other pieces of information. The authorities received so much data that the police servers buckled under the strain of thousands of gigabytes of data and eventually crashed altogether.

The investigation went on for a year and a half. Meanwhile, the public was growing more and more outraged at the length of time it was taking to find those responsible. The problem was it was taking countless hours and resources to sift through the avalanche of data that had been sent in by the public. The police were being thorough to ensure that the investigation resulted in successful convictions. They collaborated with each other very effectively to find the few pieces of good information in the sea of duplicated or worthless images and videos.

Their diligence paid off. At the time of this writing, more than three years after the Vancouver Stanely Cup riot, police say that 268 people have been charged with a total of 814 offenses. The Crown prosecutor office also says 132 of those people have pleaded guilty so far, an incredible number for an investigation of that scope. And the police did it all despite the public crashing their servers with a massive amount of unusable information.

FINDING A BALANCE

Most of the people providing information were motivated by good intentions when they sought to help. However, when investigators aren't careful, those with information have the power to—quite literally—destroy lives. Before embarking on any kind of external appeal, you must have ways of verifying and moderating the information you disseminate and receive.

As you can see, there are potential pitfalls to open communication, such as the erroneous interpretation of the facts we saw with the Boston Marathon bombing. However, there's still huge value in public information, as evidenced by the Vancouver Stanley Cup riot. Finding the balance between the negative and positive side effects of open communication and public collaboration is key.

THE GOLDEN STATE KILLER

In the summer of 1976, a violent serial killer attacked his first victims in the state of California. His initial MO was breaking into his victims' homes, tying them up in different ways, sexually assaulting them, and vanishing into the night. Then he evolved to killing. Over the course of the next decade, he murdered at least a dozen people and raped countless more, yet he evaded detection until 2018. In some ways, he was smart and meticulous. He moved to different areas. He changed his method of operation to avoid pattern analysis. He altered the profile of his victims.

Yet in other ways, he was sloppy and careless. He left DNA behind at many of his crime scenes. He phoned his victims to taunt them years after his crimes. And then, suddenly, the crimes stopped altogether. Over the years, many teams of detectives in different jurisdictions have tried to catch him. Journalists and private detectives have created documentaries, written books, and devoted countless years to his apprehension.

So why did it take so long to catch him? Well, every time a new investigator or team became involved in the case, some of the knowledge and experience of the previous investigators was lost or not fully transferred, especially when they had moved from another area or a different sector. Standards of evidence collection and retention were not consistent, and years passed without the realization that the various jurisdictions were dealing with the same perpetrator, because communication methods were slow and inconsistent. In Robert Pickton's case, a lack of collaboration led to his capture being delayed by years. For the Golden State Killer, the same issue kept the killer from being caught for *decades*.

Eventually, the detectives involved in the case admitted that if they had only been more collaborative, they would likely have caught the killer sooner. It would have taken both internal collaboration within their own agency and external collaboration with outside sources, but they had the resources necessary to pull it off—if only they had asked for more help.

NETWORKING IS A TWO-WAY STREET

Regardless of what type of investigator you want to be, the best way to build a collaborative environment is to start building your network right away. This process starts from the day you decide you want to be an investigator. If that day has already passed, then it starts today.

This network will include anyone who can provide value to you or your investigations. For example, because I continually work on behavioral profiling cases, I collaborate with a lot of forensic and criminal psychologists. I don't wait for a profiling case to come up before I go out and try to find a psychologist. Instead, I connect with people of all skills, backgrounds, and locations. That way, I can turn to my network when I need it.

It's important to note that this goes both ways. Your relationship with your network is not a one-way street. You don't get to call on people whenever you need them, use them to your advantage, and then never return their calls when they need help. Collaboration means you help each other. Even if they never call in a favor with you, make it clear to the people in your network that you are there to help them if they need it.

You can utilize all kinds of resources to grow your network. One great place to find investigative connections is LinkedIn. Reach out to those with knowledge in your area of expertise and people outside of it too. Connect with them and see if they'd be interested in working together on future investigations—if the need comes up—and most importantly, offer them your help. A successful collaboration necessitates that everyone always gives more than they take.

You can get even more creative when you search for collaborators. For example, let's say you do a lot of counterfeit investigations. You might work with several Fortune 500 companies to help tighten up their supply chain. You'll likely be considering where they buy and sell their products online in an effort to track down counterfeits, which may expand into human trafficking and modern slavery investigations. Who would you collaborate with in that situation? Keep in mind that collaboration doesn't require that you work exclusively with other investigators.

You'd need people who understand supply chains, first of all—maybe somebody who works in the international retail space. Do you know anybody who works in retail?

Who does their ordering? Where do they ship from? How do they ship? Maybe your friend who works the floor at Forever 21 doesn't have the answers, but she can point you to her manager, who can in turn get you information on their supply chain. You have to find an "in" any way you can get it and then build your way up from there. That's how you create a network.

Start thinking actively about the kind of people you'll likely need in your network. Who do you know who can make introductions for you? Are there other investigators who already specialize in your kind of work? How do you get in touch with them and connect? You can predict ahead of time what kind of experts you'll turn to, depending on your niche.

Want to investigate fraud? Get in touch with some financial experts. Domestic abuse cases? Find a surveillance specialist and get to know the staff at your local shelters and refuges, as well as victim services workers. Cyberattacks? Make friends with tech whizzes. No matter who you are, you'll eventually need help, even if you're initially afraid to ask. This industry makes no concessions for introverted investigators. Trust me—I am one.

NETWORKING FOR INTROVERTS

For an introvert, networking can be challenging. If I'm

being perfectly honest, I find networking quite difficult. I procrastinate with it. I avoid it. I am exactly the type of investigator who would rather sit behind my keyboard, not talk to anybody, and do my job with my head down, only to be replaced by a robot in a few years' time. However, introverts can often make the best investigators, as long as you utilize your strengths.

Introverts are the best listeners. We just don't have the desire to talk a lot of the time. More outgoing investigators can struggle on this point. Extraverts, practically by definition, have more to say more of the time. They must work harder than introverts to actively listen and hone their interviewing skills. If you're an introvert, there are some areas of investigation where your quietness will be an asset. However, in areas that require a more outgoing personality, such as networking, it's important to know how to compensate for the potential obstacles your personality will put in your way.

When it comes to collaboration, however, there are no right or wrong traits or characteristics for investigators. No matter your personality type—whether introverted or extraverted—networking can be challenging. It's best to acknowledge that fact before diving in headfirst and getting too frustrated to continue forward.

I've learned to supplement my introversion with emotional intelligence, which you should do as well, regardless of your personality. In moments when you're lost for words or want to retreat into yourself, teach yourself to lean on empathy, compassion, and active listening skills. Focus on the other person. Discover their motivations. The best way to get out of your own head is by trying to see things from someone else's perspective. Being genuinely interested in the person whom you're connecting with is how you build a network based on trust, integrity, and mutual benefit. That's how you connect with people. That's how you build a network of emotionally intelligent people you can depend on.

INTERNAL COLLABORATIONS

Investigators. Analysts. Profilers. These are just a few of the groups that make up the backbone of criminal investigation, each of which can be a monumental help to the others.

Recently, an analyst and I decided to collaborate on an investigation. It was a wonderful opportunity to work with an expert who'd likely be instrumental in solving the case I was working on. However, despite my experience and expertise, I still felt an underlying concern. Would he take my investigation away from me?

Even the way I thought about it before I caught myself—

my investigation—hinted at a typical territorial mentality. Sure, I was the one who had taken the case, but the ultimate goal wasn't for me to gain glory. It was to solve the problem for the client.

Because of investigators' natural competitiveness, collaborating internally—with fellow investigators—can be a tricky business. Ultimately, we should all be working toward the same goal and the same mission, but this can make it even harder not to be competitive with each other. Natural competition doesn't mean you *can't* collaborate. It just means you should recognize the dynamics at play with industry collaborations and take the necessary precautions.

One rule I follow is don't give fellow collaborators direct access to your client. Regardless of how many people you enlist to help on a case, you should always remain as the point of contact with your client. This provides continuity for the client and ensures that all information is funneled through you so you can maintain the integrity of the investigation and your own reputation.

Also, look for a collaborator who has a different skillset than you. Use a reverse-engineering process to find who you will best collaborate with. Create a mental map of how you want the case to proceed, then find the ideal collaborator for that case, and communicate your vision carefully and clearly to them. Make sure the boundaries of their role in the case are set in stone before proceeding. This reduces the chances that you'll be stepping on each other's toes in the future.

This process should work in reverse, as well. If someone approaches you for a collaboration, you must understand that you are there to help, not steal their glory or take over the case in its entirety, unless they explicitly ask you to.

Being a trustworthy and nonegotistical person in the investigation industry will help you build your internal investigation network far and wide. If another investigator knows he or she can trust you, then they'll be happy to build a long-term relationship with you.

EXTERNAL COLLABORATIONS

Sometimes, you won't need to collaborate with anyone externally. It all depends on what outside skillsets you need. External collaboration might require something as simple as an insight into a culture or a specific geographic area.

Maybe you're working on a foreign case that requires you to have an in-depth understanding of government agencies. How does the local government work in conjunction with the federal government? Or maybe you're tracking down some young people accused of stealing merchandise. Who can tell you about the environment in local high schools in your suspect's area? The information you need won't always be available from a quick Google search or on social media. Sometimes you need a local's guidance.

With external collaborations, you may need to start with your internal network, reaching out to an investigator in a specific area. From there, your fellow investigator may be able to point you toward some locals with whom you can externally collaborate. Regardless of how you go about it, never operate under the assumption that internal and external collaborations are separate entities. They often work best when you bring them together.

This is also why it's important to build your network beyond your own town, city, or even country. You never know where your investigations may lead you. You might be taken to foreign lands you know nothing about. If you already have a connection in the region, then it will make your hunt for information that much easier.

When all else fails, encourage people to reach out to you. The more people who come to you for help from outside industries, the more connections you'll make, which is better for everyone.

USING SELF-AWARENESS TO BUILD YOUR NETWORK

Whether you've realized it or not, throughout this book, you've undergone a process of improving your self-awareness. You've focused in on who you are as a person, your skills, your personality, how you work, how you learn, what type of investigations you prefer, what you're passionate about, and how to find a mentor.

After discovering all of these facets of self-awareness, you must then build outward. Hopefully, you've already begun to build your network. You've identified potential mentors, and you're working to better yourself as an expert in your industry. Even if you feel like you haven't taken active steps to make that happen yet, you've still read this book, and that's a huge move in the right direction.

Once you have a grasp on who you are—and who you are not—it will be time to connect with others whose strengths match up with your weaker points. The secret is that somebody out there knows more than you in certain subjects. Just because someone lacks knowledge in one area doesn't mean they're not a genius at something else. As you build your network, you'll meet people who can help your clients in ways you cannot. Collaborate with them.

Talk to the people around you, even if you've never

made an effort with them before—your boss, coworkers, or friends of friends. Start with the people you already know, and work outward using online research and your current connections.

Just remember, if you want something from somebody, you should be prepared to offer something in return, such as knowledge, information, or something as small as a cup of coffee.

GETTING TO KNOW EXPERTS

Collaborating with other experts is an exercise in humility that begins with sharing a common goal. Everyone respects people who want to do good in the world. Show your potential collaborators that you go after what you want because you want to *help others* more than yourself. No matter how badly you may want or need money or a fantastic reputation, you must stay humble. If you're driven by the wrong motivations, you'll attract people into your life who do the same.

It's also important to remember that true experts are busy people. They became experts for a good reason—hard work. Recognize that the people you reach out to will need time to respond. Acknowledge that you know how valuable their time is. You shouldn't expect potential collaborators to be at your beck and call. Give them respect, time, and space, and they'll be more likely to work with you eventually.

Again, be sure to offer them something in return. When you reach out to an expert, don't forget that they will often have the same motivations as you, or some other vision that is important to them or drives them. Be clear about how their helping you could benefit their own cause or their company's vision. What are their purpose points? Maybe you're strong in those areas, or, just as useful, you know somebody who is. Let the expert know that you or someone you know can help return the favor in the future.

START WITH YOUR WEAKNESSES AND BUILD OUT FROM THERE

Your process of building networks never ends. Look at it like you're always at the beginning. Every new investigation could be the start of a new team or a new collaboration. You may not be good at building networks at first. I know I wasn't. Likewise, you may not be good at collaborating at first. However, you always have time to grow. If you act with integrity and honor, and you give more than you take, people will want to work with you. It might just take some time.

For example, let's say I'm doing an investigation on a terrorism case. I'm investigating somebody I believe may have become radicalized through social networks. The person is now linked to a larger terrorist organization. I believe the suspect is also moving money around, either electronically or through other means, in order to buy weapons meant for acts of terror.

For me, the first thing I would do in any investigation is look at what I can and can't do. What do I bring to the case in terms of my own skills? How can I move this investigation forward, and where will my weaknesses get in the way?

I know I'm good at internet investigations, so in this case, I would work on profiling the suspect. I believe this person is being radicalized online, so I feel confident I'll be able to find enough of a digital footprint to understand his personality and discover who's in his network. That process is a strong point for me.

However, since I suspect the criminals are transmitting funds across the globe through Western Union and cryptocurrencies, that means there's a financial crime element to the investigation. Although I have some expertise in financial crimes and cryptocurrencies, terrorism financing requires a different set of skills, so I'll need an internal collaboration with another investigator—somebody who specializes in terrorism financing and international organized crime.

I'll also need to account for the actual weaponry. Are they being bought in another country and shipped in? Or are they being bought in the same country, just in a different jurisdiction? Are the police aware? How are those items being purchased? Where are those items being stored? Will I need a surveillance operative? The answers to these questions will tell me what kind of experts I'll need, both internally and externally.

If the crimes are taking place in a different jurisdiction, I could try to learn their unique laws. *But wouldn't it be easier to collaborate with an attorney?* Maybe the crimes are happening in another country. *I could learn a new language, but wouldn't it make more sense to collaborate with a translator?* If the transactions are taking place online, I could build my expertise in digital transactions. *But wouldn't it be a better use of my time to find an expert in computer forensics so we can seize their computer and examine their communications?*

Regardless of how much internal and external help I get, I'll still have to do the ground work myself. If the suspect's radicalization is religion-focused, I might need to go to their place of worship and talk to the people there. I might even go to their place of employment if I sense potential issues there as well. Do I need to use my own social engineering skills to get into that place of employment, or do I need to work with somebody else who has more expertise in social engineering?

Asking these questions is how I would start my investigation. I map out the potential paths of that investigation and chart all of the areas I can handle myself and where I might find roadblocks. From there, I analyze which parts will require internal collaboration, and which will require external collaboration. Then I make a list of people I know who can help fill the gaps in my knowledge.

THE MORE YOU ENGAGE YOUR NETWORK, THE MORE VALUABLE IT BECOMES

In a successful collaboration, everybody wins. You'll not only solve more cases more efficiently, but you'll also become a connector for other people, which will only increase your value within your network.

The value of a network grows proportionately with the number of people who use the network. In other words, you're not only helping yourself by seeking out collaboration, but you're also improving the entire network as a whole. This concept is known as Metcalfe's Law. Named after Robert Metcalfe, the coinventor of the Ethernet, Metcalfe's Law originally referred to telecommunication networks, stating that a system's value was proportional to the square of the number of connected users in the network.

Think of this law in terms of a social network, like Facebook. If only five people in the whole world were on Facebook, it wouldn't provide very much value. The more people who use the platform and add content to it, the more valuable Facebook becomes.

The same holds true with your collaborative networks. The more people in your network who reach out to each other for help, the more everyone learns. The more everyone learns, the more valuable you are as individuals. The more valuable you are as individuals, the more valuable you all become as a network.

Therefore, it is imperative that you continue to learn. Investigators should be voracious consumers of information. Yes, we may be secretive by nature, and we may be territorial to a fault, but we are, at our cores, seekers of truth and information. Harness that desire. It's the heart of all investigations.

HOW TO HANDLE SUCCESS

Recently, I was contacted by a journalist considering taking on a cold-case murder file. In order to continue her investigation, she needed help retrieving some old data from the internet. It just so happened to be something I could do in less than an hour. Though she could've spent the time necessary to figure out how to do it herself, she saved hours by reaching out to an expert in her extended network—me. I was the person who could help fill her knowledge gap.

In exchange for my assistance, she knows that I'll likely call on her when I'm in a tight spot myself. In the future, I know her expertise as a prestigious and experienced journalist could be invaluable. Suddenly, I know someone with a new skillset in my network, and all it cost me was an hour of my time. Some investigators would have billed for that hour, but a world-class investigator both considers the tactical and strategic advantage in collaboration and network-building and recognizes the value in building longer-term relationships based on trust, goodwill, and mutual benefit.

You should be building a network of people you trust—people you're proud to work with. And they should feel the same way about you.

In healthy collaborations, you do what you say you'll do. You don't rip people off. You don't leak confidential information. You don't speak negatively or carelessly about your peers or other people not in your network. You act professionally, and most of all, you act with integrity. With this kind of loyalty as the keystone of your reputation, eventually people will come to you rather than you seeking them out.

When that happens, your primary charge is to be generous and stay humble. Remember your core motivations. Think back to why you wanted to become a world-class investigator in the first place and move forward from there.

Personally, I have an innate desire to help people. Being a great role model drives me. I want to change the world for the better, which I believe is possible. I want to improve this industry and reduce the barriers to entry. I want to help the next generation be better, more collaborative investigators than this current generation. That is my personal mission.

Knowing your own mission and understanding your unique values will set you apart from other investigators, especially when you stick with them throughout your journey to becoming a world-class investigator.

TO DO BEFORE MOVING ON

- Reach out to potential collaborators beyond your comfort zone.
- Consider how you can offer your help in return.
- Watch your network grow.

CONCLUSION

YOU KNOW WHAT IT TAKES...NOW WHAT?

As you read this last portion of this book, you're starting out on an exciting journey toward self-awareness, mentorship, and collaboration. You have the basic knowledge and a solid foundation upon which to build a rewarding, thrilling career as a world-class investigator.

You've discovered answers to tough questions, such as: *Who are you? What are your weaknesses? What are your strengths? What's important to you? What do you need in a mentor? How can you create a dynamic, global network of collaborators?* It doesn't matter where you are in life or how old you may be. With the answers to these questions, you now have a base to work from to build your future.

From this day forward, I challenge you to be discerning and curious with everything in life. Chase after the truth, make conscious decisions, and listen to others. Most importantly, *do not stop learning.* The words and skills you take away from this book are merely a stepping-stone in your journey toward becoming a world-class investigator. Allow yourself to evolve, and be patient with your results— you may not progress at the same speed as your peers.

Never underestimate your ability to expand your reach. You can help one person or millions just by learning and communicating. Remember, you're here for a reason. It's your turn to challenge the industry's standards.

The generation gap is widening. Changes in privacy and security, combined with technological developments, mean the industry is evolving at an exponential rate. As an investigator, you have a moral responsibility to evaluate data and its sources with a human eye without completely outsourcing analysis to machines. It's our job to maintain the humanity of our industry by practicing empathy and compassion for all people.

The next generation of investigators has more opportunity and power to change the world for the better than any generation before. The technology is right there at our fingertips for immediate and widespread collaboration, collective problem-solving, the quantum processing of data, and mentorship from some of the best minds in the world. You just have to reach out and make it happen.

Remember that there's no right or wrong personality for investigations. As this book ends, I want you to leave with a strong sense of self, yet a detachment from ego. I want you to be aware of your biases and passions, all while maintaining your readiness to learn and share. Self-awareness is key. As long as you know the boundaries of your morals, ethics, and values—and you stick to them—no challenge can sway you from your path.

We're all working toward a greater good. The purpose of any investigation is to help someone in crisis or need, whether it's an individual being stalked, a corporation whose critical information has been leaked, or a criminal cold case that needs a new set of eyes to bring closure and justice to a family. Once you understand who you are and why you do what you do, you have the most important elements under control, and you can expand your toolkit from there.

Be prepared to step out into the world and explore, collaborate, and consume as much knowledge and experience as you can. Due to the nature of investigative work, going at it alone can make you distrustful, suspicious, and cynical. You'll deal with so much confidential information that you may become protective, leading to an unwillingness to collaborate. Everybody has something to teach you. Build relationships—not just because they can benefit you, but also because you can learn something from each other and find a way to make the world better together.

If we set aside our differences and learn to place more value on collaboration and on the greater good of humanity, we can do amazing things. We can work together to prevent the spread of human trafficking and modern slavery. We can prevent terror attacks. We can curb the spread of stalking and intimate partner abuse. As cliché as it sounds, we can do anything if we work together.

At this industry's heart is collaboration, yet so many people disregard it. There's so much crossover necessary within the investigation industry—from science and law enforcement to arts and culture—that collaboration should be the standard. But it's not. Without leaning on each other, this industry cannot grow. Seek mentorship. Seek collaborators. Seek experts. Grow yourself through your network, and the industry will grow with you.

You're joining a profession that gives you a direct and immediate opportunity to help people on a large scale. But you can't do it alone. Mentorship and collaboration are more accessible than ever, but you have to be prepared to take those vital first steps. That's why I've developed the World-Class Investigator Community. At

WorldClassInvestigator.com you can listen to my podcast, which dives into the subjects in this book more deeply; join a global community of investigators just like you; and find more information about my exclusive mentorship program. There's no better investment than an investment in yourself.

ACKNOWLEDGMENTS

Thank you to my friends and family, to my colleagues and peers, to the cast and crew of *Hunted*, and to all of the business mentors who have inspired, encouraged, and supported me throughout my journey.

Thank you all.

ABOUT THE AUTHOR

 **JULIE CLEGG** is a licensed investigator with more than twenty years of experience in law enforcement and professional investigations. She is an intelligence expert on the UK reality TV series *Hunted* and *Celebrity Hunted*, and she has taught investigative skills and procedures in more than twenty countries. Julie is founder and CEO of Human-i Intelligence Services, Inc. and the creator of the World-Class Investigator suite of products and services, both of which provide collaboration and mentorship services for professional investigators. She volunteers as an ambassador for Embrace UK, a nonprofit that provides support for young victims of serious crime and their families. You can find more information about the World-Class Investigator Community at WorldClassInvestigator.com.

CPSIA information can be obtained
at www.ICGtesting.com
Printed in the USA
LVHW091404020721
691769LV00004B/46